2—

DOTCOM SECRETS

"A simple process that ANY company can use to geometrically improve their traffic, conversion, and sales online."
—Tony Robbins

DOTCOM
SECRETS

THE UNDERGROUND PLAYBOOK
FOR GROWING YOUR COMPANY ONLINE

RUSSELL BRUNSON

New York

DOTCOM SECRETS

THE UNDERGROUND PLAYBOOK FOR GROWING YOUR COMPANY ONLINE

© 2015 **RUSSELL BRUNSON**.

Published in New York, New York, by Morgan James Publishing. Morgan James and The Entrepreneurial Publisher are trademarks of Morgan James, LLC. www.MorganJamesPublishing.com

The Morgan James Speakers Group can bring authors to your live event. For more information or to book an event visit The Morgan James Speakers Group at www.TheMorganJamesSpeakersGroup.com.

A **free** eBook edition is available with the purchase of this print book.

CLEARLY PRINT YOUR NAME ABOVE IN UPPER CASE

Instructions to claim your free eBook edition:
1. Download the BitLit app for Android or iOS
2. Write your name in **UPPER CASE** on the line
3. Use the BitLit app to submit a photo
4. Download your eBook to any device

ISBN 978-1-63047-477-5 paperback
ISBN 978-1-63047-478-2 eBook
Library of Congress Control Number: 2014919068

Cover Design by:
Rob Secades

Interior Design by:
Bonnie Bushman
bonnie@caboodlegraphics.com

Illustrations by:
Vlad Babich

Cover Photography:
Brandan Fisher

In an effort to support local communities and raise awareness and funds, Morgan James Publishing donates a percentage of all book sales for the life of each book to Habitat for Humanity Peninsula and Greater Williamsburg.

Get involved today, visit
www.MorganJamesBuilds.com

Habitat
for Humanity®
Peninsula and
Greater Williamsburg
Building Partner

DEDICATION

To my dad, who helped inspire me to become an entrepreneur.

To my mom, who always knew my true worth.

And to my wife, Collette, for supporting me through all of my crazy ideas, and running our home in a way that has allowed me to chase my dreams.

TABLE OF CONTENTS

ACKNOWLEDGEMENTS

There are so many people I want to thank for being willing to share their ideas with me. Ideas that ultimately became the strategies behind everything inside of this book. I also want to thank my team—all the people who helped me to implement these ideas, find out which ones work, and share them with the world.

While there are hundreds of marketers I have learned from, there are many people who gave me very specific ideas that built the framework for my company, and also for this book. I've tried to give credit to the original sources when possible, but some of these people may be left out. So I want to mention a few of the brilliant marketers who have inspired me in no particular order.

Mark Joyner, Dan Kennedy, Bill Glazer, Daegan Smith, Tony Robbins, Don Lapre, John Alanis, Andre Chaperon, Ben Settle, Steve Gray, Ryan Deiss, Perry Belcher, Armand Morin, Jason Fladlien, Ted Thomas, Mike Filsaime, David Frey, Chet Holmes, Jeff Walker,

John Reese, Robbie Summers and everyone else who has taken the risk to be an online entrepreneur and provide value online!

Lastly, I want to thank my team. These people have given me the ability to try all of these crazy ideas, and share in the successes and the losses. There have been hundreds of employees who have come through our doors, and it would be impossible to mention all of them. But I want to make special thanks to my partners who have supported me and put in so much more than time.

Brent Coppieters and John Parkes for running my companies. Todd Dickerson and Dylan Jones for creating ClickFunnels and giving us the ability to make this process simple for everyone. Dorel Nechifor for taking the risk on me when I first got started and making it possible to build my company. And Julie Eason for braving this book with me. Your countless hours have made this book possible.

WHAT THE 'ONLINE MARKETING WIZARD FRATERNITY' DOESN'T WANT YOU TO KNOW (AND: IS THIS BOOK A 'FRAUD'?)

by Dan S. Kennedy

Yes, there IS an 'online marketing wizard fraternity'. Many of them hang out together, scheme together, and work together. And yes, there ARE a few things they'd rather you *didn't* think about, while they perform their wizardly shows. This book is the first of its kind to actually reveal what is really happening behind-the-scenes in their fast-growing companies.

Don't misunderstand. Few of these wizards are actually *evil*. Most bring valid 'magic tricks' to the show. Many do guide business people to treasure. But often there is a discernible pattern behind everything they say, teach, promise, and promote: a deliberately-engineered and exacerbated lack of solid ground. This book doesn't just focus on magic tricks, but the core strategies you have to have in place to scale a company with online media.

It is in the wizard's best interest for you to believe everything in the online media, marketing and business world is shiny and new, constantly changing, and un-tethered from the old rules, principles, facts, and math of successful advertising and marketing.

This book by Russell Brunson is different. While teaching you about the "shiny" secrets of the Internet, he shows you how to build these tactics and strategies into your business on solid ground—tactics and strategies founded in true direct-response marketing. It is **your responsibility** to resist the seduction of short-lived, bright and shiny lures, popularity and peer pressure, and the siren-songs of superficially knowledgeable promoters of 'new' tactics with no knowledge of its original direct response genealogy. **You** must exercise discernment.

I'm *for* challenging norms and breaking rules. But I also like solid ground, not ever-shifting sand. I like being confident and in control of things—particularly my money and the making of it—not in constant high-anxiety and at the mercy of wizards.

I taught myself direct marketing as a *science*. I'm a reliability guy. I'm far more interested in a car that starts and runs well and predictably every time you turn the key than one that looks sexy and is popular with some in-crowd, but might stall at 80 MPH or not start at all. I like evergreen, not frequently obsolete. In my roles as a strategic consultant and a direct-response copywriter, I am all about creating advertising, marketing, and sales *assets* of lasting value for my clients—not moneymaking devices written in disappearing ink.

That's why I agreed to write the foreword for *this* online marketing wizard's book. I admire the truth Russell has put between these pages.

Unlike many of these wiz kids, Russell Brunson is grounded in direct marketing *disciplines*.

Discipline is good. General Norm Schwarzkopf (of Operation Desert Storm fame) once said:

"Shined shoes save lives."

Norm went on to explain that in the heat of battle, the fog of war, under pressure, *the undisciplined die.* So it is in business. I sit now, as infrequently as possible, in meetings with young online marketing people demonstrably devoid of any disciplined thinking. They are full of opinion and youthful hubris but very short on facts. I would not want to share a foxhole with them or depend on them. I would risk it with Russell.

This book offers solid ground in the very ethereal world of online marketing and commerce. It properly treats Internet media *as media—* not as a business. It utilizes the science of split-testing. It builds on long-proven marketing funnel and sales architecture. It takes a very disciplined approach.

It is, in one way only, a *fraudulent* book. The title is deceptive. It really is not about "*dot com* secrets" nor is it a playbook for "growing your company *online.*" It is that, but such a narrowed and limiting characterization is deceptive.

In truth, this is a *solid* book about *reliable* marketing 'secrets' that can be applied to 'dot com' business activities—and that are 'secrets' to many who've come of age only paying attention to what they see occurring online. In truth, this is a *proven* playbook for growing your company with effective lead generation and sales/conversion methods, which can be used online and offline.

'Solid' and 'reliable' and 'proven' aren't the sexiest positioning terms, so Russell can be forgiven for holding them back, waiting to reveal them inside the book, carefully. 'Growing Your Company ONLINE' sounds cooler and less work than 'Growing Your Company', so he can also be forgiven for playing to peoples' fascination of the moment. He is a wizard, and as such must be permitted some legerdemain. But let's you and I be very clear about reality. Let me serve a useful purpose for you here.

My advice: Don't settle for or be distracted by mere tricks. Be a responsible *adult*. Invest your time 'n treasure in information, skill and properties that can yield harvest after harvest after harvest—not fleeting fads, not sexy ideas that age very poorly. And don't fall for the idea that any new media gets to defy gravity and live un-tethered to reality, math, or history.

Don't go into this book in lust for a new, cool, quick, easy "fix" or nifty "toy" or clever gimmick that might make you money today but require you to find another and another and another, at frantic pace.

Go into this book in search of deep understanding and profound clarity about the structure and science of effective marketing to be applied in the online media universe.

—Dan S. Kennedy

Dan S. Kennedy is a trusted strategic advisor to hundreds of 7-figure income professionals, direct marketing pros, and CEOs. He is also the author of over 20 books, including *No B.S. Guide to Ruthless Management of People and Profits* (2nd Edition). Information about Dan at: www.NoBSBooks.com and www.GKIC.com.

WHAT THIS BOOK IS ABOUT
(AND WHAT IT'S NOT ABOUT)

Hey, my name is Russell Brunson . . .

Before we get started, I want to introduce myself and let you know what this book is about (and more importantly, what it's not about).

This book is NOT about getting more traffic to your website—yet the "DotComSecrets" I'm going to share with you will help you to get exponentially MORE traffic than ever before.

This book is NOT about increasing your conversions—yet these DotComSecrets will increase your conversions MORE than any headline tweak or split test you could ever hope to make.

If you are currently struggling with getting traffic to your website, or converting that traffic when it shows up, you may think you've got a traffic or conversion problem. In my experience, after working with thousands of businesses, I've found that's rarely the case. Low traffic and weak conversion numbers are just symptoms of a much greater problem, a problem that's a little harder to see (that's the bad news), but a lot easier to fix (that's the good news).

Recently, I had a chance to fly to San Diego to work with Drew Canole from FitLife.tv. He had built a following of 1.2 million followers on Facebook, but because of some changes at Facebook, his traffic had dropped by 90%. He was now spending $116 to sell a $97 product. He was no longer profitable.

Drew's team called me because they wanted help with two things: traffic and conversions.

I smiled because that's why most people call me. They usually assume that I'm going to help them tweak a headline or change their ad targeting, and solve their problems. But I knew that, like most companies I work with, FitLife.tv's problem wasn't a traffic or conversion problem.

It rarely is.

More often than not, it's a FUNNEL problem.

After listening to Drew and his team share with me all of their numbers, their pains and frustrations, and their ups and downs, I sat back in my chair and told them they were in luck.

"You don't have a traffic or conversion problem," I said.

"What are you talking about? Our traffic is down 90%, and we can't break even converting our customers!" Drew said.

"The problem is you can't spend enough to acquire a customer, and the way to fix that problem is to fix your sales funnel," I replied calmly.

One of my mentors, Dan Kennedy, says, *"Ultimately, the business that can spend the most to acquire a customer wins."*

The reason Drew's business wasn't making money was because he wasn't able to spend enough to acquire a customer. If we fix his sales funnel so that instead of making $97 for every $116 he spends, he can start making two to three times as much money for each sale—and then the whole game changes. Suddenly, he can afford to buy more traffic from more places; he can outbid his competitors, and he can spend two to three times more than he is now, all while becoming exponentially more profitable.

So, what changes did we make to Drew's business? How did we take a sales funnel that was losing money and transform it into a tool that allowed FitLife.tv to spend MORE money than its competitors, while gaining more traffic, more customers, and more sales?

THAT is what this book is about.

This book will take you on a journey similar to the one I took Drew and his team on. It will help you understand how to structure your company's products and services in a way that will allow you to make two to three times as much money from the same traffic that you're getting now. And when you follow the steps, you'll open the floodgates, allowing you to spend a lot more money to get a lot more new customers.

This book will also show you how to communicate with your customers in a way that makes them naturally want to ascend up your ladder of offerings and give you more money as you provide them more value.

Once you know the foundational concepts behind DotComSecrets, we'll dive into the phases of a sales funnel and explore the building blocks you will need to use in each phase.

Finally, I will give you the seven core sales funnels I use in all my companies, plus all of the sales scripts we use to convert people at each stage in those funnels. You can choose to copy my proven funnels and scripts as is, or you may tweak them to better fit your particular business.

When you implement each of these secrets, you will transform your business and your website from a flat, two-dimensional company into a three-dimensional sales and marketing machine that allows you to outspend your competitors, acquire an almost unlimited number of new customers, make (and keep) more money, and most importantly, serve more people.

That is what this book is about.

INTRODUCTION

My junk mail addiction began when I was twelve years old. I remember the exact night my obsession with junk mail and direct response marketing started. My dad was up late watching TV while working on a project. Normally, he made me go to bed early, but that night he let me stay up late and watch TV with him. I wasn't as interested in the news as I was in spending time with my dad.

When the news ended, I was waiting for him to send me to bed, but he didn't, so I started watching what came on next. It was one of those late night infomercials. This particular infomercial featured a guy named Don Lapre who was explaining how to make money with "tiny little classified ads." I'm not sure why he grabbed my attention. Maybe, because I was so young, I didn't understand that making money fast "wasn't possible." Maybe my fascination grew because he was so charismatic. Whatever the reason, as soon as he started talking, I was hooked.

During this infomercial, he told stories about how he started his first business. He explained how he came up with an idea for a product and then placed a classified ad in his local newspaper to sell this new product. The first week after his ad ran, he made enough money to pay for the ad and was left with about thirty dollars in profit. While most people wouldn't consider that a big win, Don knew that he could take that same winning ad, run it in other newspapers, and make a thirty-dollar profit from each paper.

He ended up running that ad in thousands of newspapers and made tens-of-thousands of dollars a month doing it!

I didn't realize it at the time, but Don was teaching me (and everyone else who was watching) the basics of direct response marketing, which could be applied to any company.

Well, as you can guess, my twelve-year-old eyes opened wide, and my heart started racing. I remember getting so excited that I couldn't sleep that night—or the rest of the week. All I could think about was buying Don's system so I could start making money. I asked my dad if he would help me pay for it, but as any good father should, he made me go out and work for the money. I mowed lawns, weeded gardens, and worked really hard for three or four weeks to earn the money to buy the system.

I still remember calling the 1-800 number to order. When the box showed up, my heart was racing as I ripped it open. I started reading the pages as Don explained to me the basics of direct response marketing.

And that is where this journey began for me.

After that, I started collecting classified ads and calling the 1-800 numbers on them to see what people would send me. I started to see that other companies were doing the same thing that Don was teaching!

Then I started to look at magazines and saw the same types of ads. So I would call the phone numbers and send in for the free "info-kits" that these ads were promoting as well.

Within three or four weeks, I started getting "junk mail." (I put *junk mail* in quotation marks because studying that junk mail has literally made me millions.) I started getting so much mail that the mailman couldn't physically fit it all into the mailbox. I would come home from junior high school, and my parents might have two or three letters, but I'd have a whole stack of my very own mail. I'd take it all into my bedroom and read through every letter. I didn't know it at the time, but I was reading long-form sales letters from some of the greatest direct response marketers of all time. I saw what they were doing and how they were doing it, and it was fascinating to me.

Whatever they were selling, the process was the same. They would place a small ad asking people to contact their company for a free report. After you contacted them, they would send you a sales letter, disguised as a free report, selling a low-ticket information product. When I purchased the product, they would send me their "system"—along with another sales letter selling me a high-ticket product (fig. 0.1).

THE OFFLINE METHOD

Fig 0.1 The offline sales funnels brought prospects through a predictable series of steps.

This was my first exposure to sales funnels. I didn't know it at the time, but this process I was seeing over and over again offline would become the exact SAME system that I would use to grow hundreds of companies online.

Now, while funnels often get much more advanced than this, look at this diagram to see what offline funnels look like, and note how similar they are to the online funnels I will be showing you throughout this book (fig. 0.2):

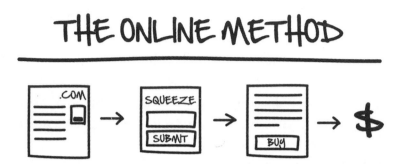

Fig 0.2 Today's online sales funnels are practically identical to the offline direct response marketing funnels I studied as a kid.

Looking back, I think it's funny that while most kids my age were collecting baseball cards, I was studying junk mail and learning marketing funnels. When I left for college, my mom made me throw my junk mail in the garbage, but I got this one last picture with the best marketing and sales education I could have ever received.

Unfortunately, I was never able to afford to sell stuff through classified ads and direct mail when I was twelve.

Not your typical teenager!

But I understood the concept. It wasn't until ten years later, during my sophomore year in college, that I re-discovered direct response marketing and saw how I could use it on the Internet.

MY FIRST ONLINE BUSINESS

One late night during my sophomore year in college, I was lying in bed—way too tired to turn off the TV. So instead, I flipped through the channels, and one commercial caught my eye. It was explaining how people were "making money online with a website." I knew I needed to learn more. I dialed the number, got a ticket for a local event, and the next night I was at a seminar in a local Holiday Inn. That little seminar re-ignited my interest in business and direct response marketing. I remember hearing the speakers talk about how people were using the Internet to make money in a way that was almost identical to what I

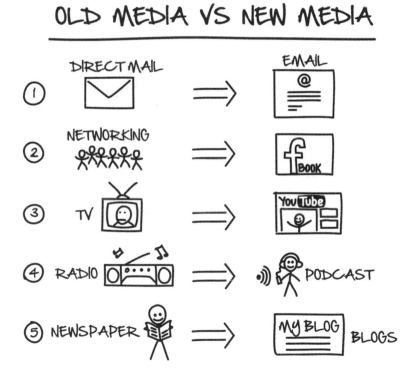

Fig 0.3 Blogs, podcasts, and online video are simply newer versions of the old-school offline media channels.

had learned when I was a kid. But instead of using mail, they were using email; instead of using magazines, they had blogs; instead of the radio, they were using podcasts. It was fascinating, and I was hooked from Day One.

I started looking at other people's websites, studying how these businesses were making money. I decided to model what I saw. After all, if it worked for them, it could work for me. So I created similar products and services to what others were selling online. My websites looked similar and the copy on the pages was similar, but for some reason, my efforts made very little (if any) money. I was frustrated because I could see others making money successfully. What was I doing wrong?

It took almost two full years of studying, researching, and interviewing successful marketers before I realized that what I was seeing online wasn't the full business. The people who were making money were doing it through steps and processes invisible to the naked eye.

While I had modeled the part of their businesses that I could see, there were multiple funnels happening behind the scenes that made the magic work. I found that the difference between a ten-thousand-dollar website and a ten-million-dollar company was all of the things happening AFTER a buyer came into the initial funnel.

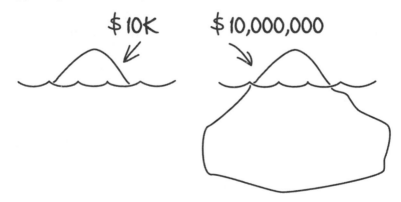

Fig 0.4 I was modeling what I could see happening on the surface, but the real money was made in ways I couldn't see.

It took me years to discover and master these DotComSecrets—but when I did, my company quickly went from a few hundred dollars a month to millions of dollars a year in revenues.

I wanted to write this book, not because I'm smarter than anyone else, but because I think there are a lot of people like I was. People who model the surface level of what others are doing and are frustrated that they aren't getting similar results. This book is the culmination of a decade spent analyzing hundreds of companies and their successful sales funnels. I have built over one hundred sales funnels of my own and have worked with thousands of students and clients to build funnels in every market you can dream of—both online and offline.

I hope that after reading this book you will realize your dreams of success are a lot closer than you think. You will soon see that by providing a ton of value, communicating effectively with your audience, and building out your sales processes in a very strategic way, you can get your product, service, or message out to the world. And, you can get paid what you're worth while doing it.

THREE WAYS THIS BOOK IS DIFFERENT

By purchasing this book, you have put your trust in me as your coach. I know that you're busy; I fully understand and respect that. It's important for you to know that I will not waste your time. You have many choices in business and success training, and I'm honored that you've decided to spend your valuable time with me. Here's how this book is different from other business books you may have read:

1. Everything I Show You in this Book Is Evergreen. If you've tried to learn how to grow your company online in the past, you've probably purchased books and courses with systems that worked when they were created, but became outdated before they even got to the publisher. When Google changes an algorithm or Facebook introduces a new layout, many tactics suddenly become obsolete.

This book, on the other hand, is a playbook for creating marketing funnels that will exponentially increase your sales online. It is an evergreen guide. It will be as useful ten years from now as it is today. I only focus on strategies and concepts that will remain the same—even when technology changes.

2. I Don't Just Teach This Stuff; I Actually Do It. There are a ton of people teaching Internet marketing, and the vast majority of them make money by teaching other people the Internet marketing strategies they learned about online. Dan Kennedy calls those people "shovel sellers" because during the gold rush, the people who made the most money were the ones selling the shovels. Today's "shovel sellers" are selling you Internet marketing strategies without actually using any of the strategies themselves.

The difference between me and most of my competitors is that *I actually do this, for real.* That's right. I use every one of the secrets I'm about to reveal to you. And I've tried them in dozens of different markets—from supplements to coaching to software. I also work directly with hundreds of other businesses, advising them and increasing their profitability in almost every niche and every industry you can dream of.

About seven or eight years ago, I had the good fortune to work with direct marketing legends Dan Kennedy and Bill Glazer. They work with entrepreneurs all around the world, and I was their main Internet marketing trainer for almost six years. This was a very unique situation, and I was able to work with hundreds of offline businesses, teaching them to implement the same concepts I'm about to share with you.

I've also had a chance to teach these DotComSecrets at Tony Robbins' Business Mastery seminar as well. I can tell you from experience that these strategies work for both online and offline businesses in just about any industry you can think of. Throughout the book, I'll share examples of these different types of businesses so you can see how each strategy could work in any market.

The book is divided into several sections. Sections 1, 2, and 3 are going to give you the core concepts that you MUST understand before you can create your first marketing funnel. Once you understand the secrets behind what makes online selling work, I will teach you how to build your own sales funnels.

Section 4 describes the many different sales funnels we use in our companies every day. It also gives you the sales scripts you need to move people through your marketing funnel so they will purchase from you.

Section 5 will show you some of the easier ways to implement all the technology involved. I see people get tripped up by the tech all the time. So I want you to skip the hard stuff and make it easy on yourself.

Once you know how funnels work, implementing them is a simple matter of picking which one you want to use and setting it up. Please don't skip ahead to the Funnels and Scripts section until you've read the earlier chapters, or you will miss learning the core strategies that make those funnels and scripts work. I want everything to make total sense to you.

3. Image Recall. Throughout the book, you're going to notice tons of simple little diagrams. At first, they won't make sense to you. But after you read through the chapter or section, you'll get it. I promise. The reason the pictures are so basic is because I want you to be able to look at the image and immediately recall the concepts. The graphics are engineered for instant recall. At some point in the future, if you need to remember how to structure an upsell sales letter or a two-step consulting funnel, you'll be able to pull out the picture and instantly recall how to do it. When you need that image recall, you can flip through the book to find the pictures, if you like. Or you can go to www.DotComSecretsBook.com/resources/diagrams and print them out. I like to keep a notebook of all the pictures of funnels and scripts I develop, so I can always find the one I need. I even have some students who have certain images taped to their office walls as memory aids.

I recommend reading through the entire book once from beginning to the very end. You're uncovering the rest of the iceberg, and you need to understand the concepts in order. Once you've gone through all the material, then you can go back to the chapters you know will make a big difference right away.

I'm excited for you to dive in and have some fun with this. So, let's get started!

LADDERS
AND FUNNELS

SECRET #1:

THE SECRET FORMULA

THE SECRET FORMULA

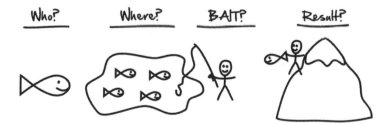

Who?   Where?   BAIT?   Result?

t was 11:27 a.m. on a Monday morning, and no matter what I told myself, I just couldn't get out of bed. The muscles in my body ached, although it didn't make sense. I knew I wasn't sore from exercise because I hadn't worked out. I had a sick feeling in my stomach that felt like the flu, but I knew I wasn't sick. In my head, I was WISHING that I had a boss, so he could fire me and end this nightmare that I knew I had to face as soon as I finally stumbled out of bed.

How had I gotten here? Just a few years earlier, I had "officially" become an entrepreneur and launched my own company. And despite a lot of mistakes along the way, I had learned a few tricks and was having success. The company I started was profitable. We were serving people and making a difference, but for some reason, I was miserable.

A few weeks later, I found myself in front of a huge, blank whiteboard trying to sketch out why I was feeling this way. Something was wrong with my business, and I wanted to figure out what it was. After what seemed like hours, I wrote down two words:

Who?

Result?

I asked myself, "WHO is the person I really want to work with?" Up to that point in my business, I had been trying to sell to anyone and everyone I could. While that sounds smart at first, it left me tired, frustrated, and empty inside.

After I got a good idea of WHO I would ideally work with if I had that choice, I started to think about the RESULT I would want to give them. I asked myself, "Where could I serve my customer at the highest level?" I realized it wasn't through a product or a service. Rather, it was by giving them a result that would change their lives. That result is where I wanted to take them.

A few minutes later, I added two more words to the board:

Where?

Bait?

WHERE are these people? How can I find them online? What type of BAIT can I create to attract my dream client and repel everyone else?

These questions eventually became the outline for what I now call "The Secret Formula," and it's really the first step that you HAVE to take before you can grow any company.

THE SECRET FORMULA

The secret formula consists of four simple questions. These are the same four questions that I ask anyone who hires me for personal consultations. At the time of writing, companies pay me twenty-five thousand dollars per day to help them understand and implement this formula and the funnels and scripts inside of this book. Now while I know you didn't pay anywhere near twenty-five thousand to learn this information and go through this process, I recommend you treat this and all of the exercises inside of this book as if you did invest the full amount. If you do, you will get a lot more out of the process I'm going to take you through, and this book will become like a private, twenty-five thousand dollar consultation with me. Okay, let me walk you through the process.

Question #1: Who Is Your Dream Client? The first question you have to ask yourself is, *Who do I actually want to work with?* Most of us start with a product idea, never thinking about who we want as clients, customers, vendors, and associates. But these are the people you will be interacting with day in and day out. You'll probably spend more time with these people than your own friends and family. You choose your significant other carefully, so why wouldn't you take the same time and care in deciding who your dream client or customer will be? If you're just getting started, this may not seem important. But I promise you that if you don't consciously choose your dream client, one day you will wake up like I did, working with people who exhaust you and wishing that someone could fire you from the business you created.

After I had successfully launched my first software company, a lot of people took notice of my success online and started asking me how I was making money. Because I saw the demand, I thought it would be fun to teach others how to start their own businesses online.

The good thing was there were a LOT of people who wanted to start businesses, and we made a lot of money teaching them. But the downside was that most of them didn't have any money (and couldn't invest in the higher-ticket things I wanted to sell). And most had no business experience, so I had to spend tons of time on the fundamentals, and that drove me crazy (which is why I didn't want to get out of bed in the mornings). I had so much value *I wanted* to provide people—showing how I had scaled my companies, teaching conversion secrets and how we structure our funnels—but 99% of my time was spent showing them how to buy a domain and set up hosting.

I literally spent years serving these customers, and it made me miserable. My family suffered, and no matter how much money we made, I wasn't happy. It took years before I sat back and actually thought about the WHO. I realized I had overlooked some pretty important questions:

Who are my dream clients?

What do they look like?

What are they passionate about?

What are their goals, dreams, and desires?

After about a week of thinking about the WHO question, I sat down and created two customer avatars: one for the men I wanted to work with and one for the women I wanted to work with.

For the women, I picked a name and wrote it down: Julie. Then I listed out the things I knew about Julie. She is successful and driven; she has a message to share; she values her personal growth over money; and she's already grown her business to at least five figures a year.

Next, I wrote down the name Mike. Next to Mike's name, I wrote out the things I knew about Mike. He is a former athlete. At some point, he has helped to change someone's life in a small way and wants to learn how to help more people. He values growth over money, and he's already built his business to at least five figures a year.

Then I went to Google images and typed in *Julie* and the characteristics I had written out. Within minutes, I found a picture that looked like the women in my mind. I printed it out and hung it on my wall. I did the same for Mike, and within minutes, I had both pictures of my dream clients hanging on my wall.

This may seem like a silly exercise, but it's important that you do it anyway. Really spend some time thinking about who you want to work with. Write out their characteristics and then go find an actual picture to represent them. It's amazing how your perspective changes when you have a physical picture of your ideal customer—instead of a hazy, half-formed image in your head.

Question #2: Where Can You Find Them? The next question in the Secret Formula is WHERE can you find this ideal man or woman? Where do they hang out online? Are they on Facebook or Instagram? What groups are they part of? What email newsletters do they subscribe to? What blogs do they read? Are they reading *The New York Times* or *The Huffington Post*? What other interests do they have? Do they like sports or the arts? How about fishing or race cars? If you don't know the *who*, it will be hard to find out *where* your perfect client can be found. So make sure you know exactly who you're trying to attract. Then just write down a few places you think the prospect might hang out online. Over the next few chapters, we're going to take a deep dive into how and where to find your dream clients. I'll show you exactly where to find the people you're looking for.

Question #3: What Bait Will You Use to Attract Them? Once we know *where* the dream customers are, we have to create the right bait to attract them. Your bait could be a physical book, a CD, DVD, or an audio recording—anything that your dream customer would pay attention to and want. As my company moved away from selling to beginners and toward attracting dream clients, our first step was to create new bait that would attract "Mike" or "Julie."

So we created a book called *DotComSecrets Labs: 108 Proven Split Test Winners*. This bait worked great for us, because most beginners don't know what a split test is. But we KNEW that Julie and Mike (our DREAM customers) would know what these terms mean and they would be hungry to get their hands on the book. Within days of launching this new offer, we had thousands of dream clients lining up to work with us. When you find out what your dream clients want, it becomes very easy to attract them. Throughout this book, we're going to talk more about creating the right bait. Right now, just realize the bait has to match what your dream customer wants.

Question #4: What Result Do You Want To Give Them? Once you've hooked your dream customers with the perfect bait, the last question is what RESULT do you want to give them? I'm not talking about what product or service you want to sell them. A business is NOT about products and services. A business is about what *result* you can get for your clients. Once you (and they) understand that concept, then price is no longer a barrier.

For me, I knew that the *best* way I can serve my dream client is to send my team to their office and help build out their sales funnels, hire and train their sales team, and set up systems to drive consistent leads into the company. That is how I can have the deepest impact and serve the client at the highest level. Ideally, it's where I would like to take all of my customers. That type of service is *not* cheap, but the results I can deliver at that level are amazing. To put it in perspective, for that service, my company charges a retainer and a percentage of sales, which combined equal one million dollars.

I understand that many of my customers won't be able to pay me for that level of service (which is why we develop other products and services), but understanding where you ultimately want to take the dream client is the key to this step.

Imagine that your clients could pay you anything to get a desired result. What, then, would you do to help guarantee their success? Where would you lead them? What does that place look like? Keep that place in your mind; it's the pinnacle of success for your clients. It's where you want to take them, and it's the key to this last step.

That's it. The four steps again are as follows:

1. Who are your dream clients?
2. Where can you find them??
3. What bait will you use to attract them?
4. What result do you want to give them?

I know that this exercise seems simple, but it is the key to everything else we will be discussing in this book. So take a few minutes now and really answer these four questions.

Up Next: In the next chapter, we are going to dig a little deeper and focus on the steps you need to follow to lead your dream customer from taking the "bait" to consuming your product offerings to arriving "where" you want to take them. If you structure this correctly, people will naturally ascend to where you want them to be. They will give you more money, and you'll be able to serve them at a much higher level.

THE VALUE LADDER

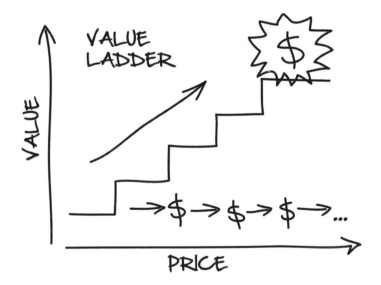

R ussell, are you a smoker?"

"What?" I responded. "No, I've never smoked in my life . . . why do you ask?"

"Well, I noticed that your teeth are turning a little yellow, and I wasn't sure if you were a smoker . . . or maybe you drink coffee?"

"No, I don't drink coffee either . . .," I said. "My teeth look that yellow!?"

Those were the first words my new dentist said to me about 10 minutes into our first appointment.

When I started my new business a few years earlier, my wife and I had no insurance of any kind. I was just hustling to sell things online to try and put food on the table.

Then about four or five years into my business, I started hiring employees. What I didn't realize when I first hired them was most "real" companies give their employees benefits. Because I had never had a real job before, I wasn't really sure what benefits were (besides hanging out with me all day, which I assumed was the best benefit ever!). No, they wanted health insurance and dental insurance. So I decided to cave and get them all a "benefits" package. Within days of getting our new dental insurance, I got a postcard in the mail offering a free teeth cleaning.

"Sweet! We've got insurance. It's a free cleaning. I'm in."

And that's where it all started . . .

Within minutes, the dentist commented on my "yellow" teeth.

"No, I don't drink coffee or smoke. Are they really yellow?"

"Yeah, they are. But don't worry. If you want, I can go out back and make some custom teeth-whitening trays for you. You'll have to use them for a few weeks, but if you follow the system, your teeth will be white again."

Well, I'm sure you know what my response was . . .

"Yes, please! I don't want yellow teeth."

The dentist kept working on my teeth, and a little while later, he said, "So, did you have braces when you were a kid?"

"Yeah, I did. How can you tell?"

"Well, your two bottom teeth are shifting again, and that usually happens to people who had braces."

"My teeth are shifting? Seriously? What can you do about that?"

"Well, if you want, I can build a retainer for you, which will help keep your teeth in place."

"Yes, please!"

When I walked into the dentist office that morning, I had come in for a *free* teeth cleaning. And in less than an hour, I walked out paying over two thousand dollars for my whitening kit and my new retainers. This dentist had strategically taken me through a powerful process that I call a Value Ladder.

First, he had created bait (free teeth cleaning) that would attract his dream client (me).

Second, he provided value to me by cleaning my teeth and noticing that my teeth had become yellow. Because I had received value, I naturally wanted to move forward and get additional value from him.

He then found another way that he could provide value to me—the retainers—and again, I naturally took him up on that offer as well.

Now, for many dentists, they make the most money and provide the most value for their patients by offering cosmetic surgery. Luckily, I didn't need any cosmetic surgery on that visit, or I could have been out ten thousand dollars or more.

On my way out the door, the secretary scheduled me for another appointment six months later, adding me to their "continuity" program. Continuity is where you continue paying on a weekly, monthly, or yearly basis until you decide to cancel. This dentist had a perfectly executed Value Ladder (fig. 2.2).

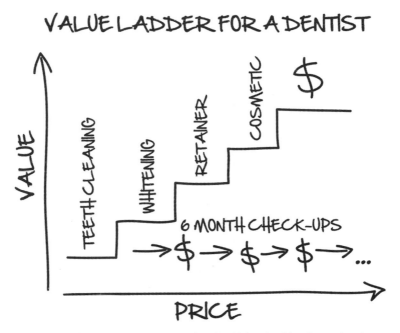

Fig. 2.2 : This is a great example of a Value Ladder for a dentist.

One of the first things I explain to people when I start working with them is the concept of a Value Ladder, and it's the first thing you have to build out *before* you can start working on any sales funnel. If you look at how we structure it, you'll see that on the left hand axis we have value, and on the bottom axis we show the price (fig. 2.3).

Now, on the top right hand corner of this graph, you'll see the big $ sign. This is *where you want to take your client.* This is where you can provide them the most value—and also charge them the most.

For dentists, this is usually cosmetic surgery. For my company, it's going into your business to build out your sales funnels, set up your backend systems, and generate leads for you. We currently charge our clients one hundred thousand dollars plus 10% of their profits (up to one million) to provide this service for them. So the total cost to my clients is a million dollars for this service. But it's the BEST thing I can provide them, and it gives me the ability to serve them at the highest level.

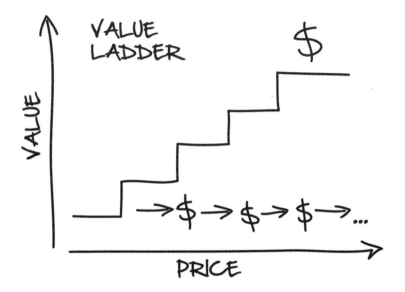

Fig. 2.3: You can use this same model to design your own Value Ladder for your business.

Now, ideally we would like to sell *everyone* our best thing, right? You want to serve your customers in the highest way possible. But the sad truth is that if I were to walk up to you on the street and say, "Give me a million dollars, and I'll help you to grow your company," you would either laugh in my face or run away, thinking I was insane.

Why is that?

It's because we just met, and so far, I haven't provided you any value.

But if you came to my website and saw that I was giving away a free book with 108 of my BEST split tests and all you had to do was cover the $9.95 shipping, do you think that you'd order it?

If you're in my target audience you would—because the price is low, and you have a chance to receive some value in a non-threatening way, allowing you to see if you like the experience. Just like I did with the dentist.

Now, if you order that book from me and receive value from it, you will naturally want more. You'll want to ascend my Value Ladder (fig. 2.3a) and see if there are other ways I can provide value for you.

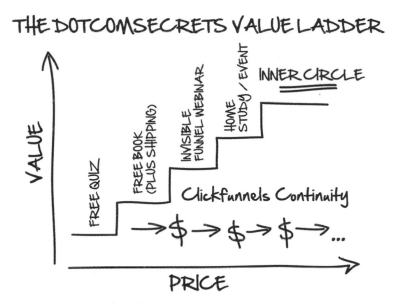

Fig. 2.3a: My DotComSecrets' Value Ladder includes products and services at all levels, including an ongoing continuity program.

You may buy one of my home study courses or attend one of my live events. If you receive value from that, then you may decide to sign up for my $10,000 Ignite program, or maybe my $25,000 Inner Circle program. And if I provide awesome value there, then you will naturally want to keep ascending . . . and THAT is how we sell our million-dollar packages. We provide insane amounts of value at each step of our Value Ladder, so our clients naturally want to ascend, get more value, and pay us more money.

Oh yeah, and just like the dentist, no Value Ladder is complete without a good continuity program. There are many ways to structure your continuity program. It could be organized around software, membership sites, or ongoing coaching, but it should be something you can bill for each month. That residual income will become the lifeblood of your business. For my DotComSecrets business, our main continuity program is our software ClickFunnels, which allows people to create sales funnels with the click of a mouse. Our clients pay us monthly to use this software to help run their businesses. It saves them a ton of time and money and provides us with residual income. Win-Win.

WHAT DOES YOUR VALUE LADDER LOOK LIKE?

Now I'm aware that everyone reading this has a different type of company. At this point, you're probably trying to figure out how the Value Ladder applies to your business. I want to share with you a story that will show you how we were able to create a Value Ladder for a business that doesn't seem to have any type of ascending products or services.

I have a chiropractor friend, Dr. Chad Woolner, whom I've known for a long time. In fact, it was his urging that got me to create this book. Like most chiropractors, he makes his living doing adjustments for about fifty dollars each. He runs ads, patients come in, get adjusted in about ten minutes, pay him fifty dollars, and leave. Sometimes, if the person has a more serious condition, Chad may put the client on a continuity plan and have them come in a few times a week over the next few months. But that's about it.

One day my friend and I were talking. He wanted to know what I would do differently in his business if I were him. I thought it over for a few days, when a funny thing happened. At the time, I was working with a group of wrestlers who were training for the Olympics. Each week a chiropractor came in and adjusted all of the wrestlers. One week, the regular doc couldn't make it in. So, instead of waiting for a week, one of the athletes jumped on YouTube, typed in "how to give a chiropractic adjustment," and watched a few videos until he felt like an expert. Then he walked into the other room and quickly adjusted everyone on the team.

Now, before I move on, I feel like I should give a disclaimer or a warning or something. ☺ Don't get me wrong. The point of this story is NOT to say you should go watch YouTube videos and then start practicing medicine! (And no emails telling me that's illegal or crazy . . . okay?) The point is that in about thirty minutes, someone with no formal training at all learned to do what we were paying the chiropractor for. I started laughing, called my chiropractor friend immediately, and told him the story.

Naturally, he wasn't as amused as I was. He launched into a long rant about why that was dangerous and why we shouldn't have done it. Then I stopped him and said, "Look, I wasn't just calling to be a jerk. I want to teach you something really powerful. You went to college for years to learn how to be a chiropractor—yet, within thirty minutes, one wrestler was able to learn EVERYTHING that you currently do in your clinic."

Silence.

"I'm curious, while you were going to school, did you learn anything else besides adjustments?"

Defensively, he started to tell me about all sorts of other things he had learned and knew how to do.

"I spent years learning nutrition and natural healing. I can help stop fibromyalgia, carpal tunnel syndrome, and . . ."

And that's where I stopped him . . .

"Have you ever provided ANY of these services to your clients? Or do you stop giving them value after the fifty dollar adjustments?"

Now I want to pause here, because most companies I work with, even if they think they have a Value Ladder, really only have *part* of one.

Almost always, I spend my time working with them on adding products and services to the front of their Value Ladders, as well as the back.

After that discussion, I sat down with my friend and we mapped out his current Value Ladder. It looked kind of like this (fig. 2.4):

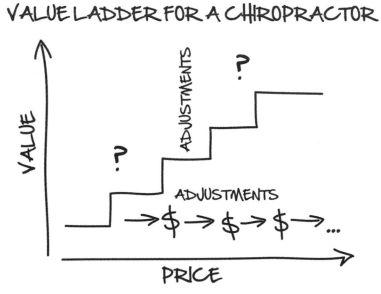

Fig. 2.4: At first, my friend only had one basic service. I helped him flesh out other offerings so he had a fully developed Value Ladder.

Then we looked at other ways he could provide more value to his clients. We figured out where he really wanted to take them. Ultimately, he created a new wellness program, for which he could charge five thousand dollars. The clients who participated would get ten times more value from each visit to his clinic. That was the backend—the highest point—of his ladder.

Then, after we built out my friend's backend Value Ladder, we still had to find an attractive frontend offer to get people through the door. A chiropractic adjustment just isn't that sexy. It's not like a massage that people enjoy getting, and it's not like going to a traditional medical doctor where you think you're going to die and need some medicine fast. People usually wait until they're in great pain before they'll come in for an adjustment. Chiropractic adjustments just aren't that exciting. If you have a blah frontend offer, your business will always struggle.

We sat down, thought through his business, and decided that a massage would be a good thing to offer as the frontend of his Value Ladder. People love getting massages, and it's bait he could use to get people into his clinic.

Now he has two full-time massage therapists who give free massages to get people in the door. And just like my dentist sells teeth whitening and retainers, these therapists are trained to feel when a person's spine or ribs are out of place and might need an adjustment. Then they upgrade the client to the adjustments and then to the wellness programs (fig. 2.5).

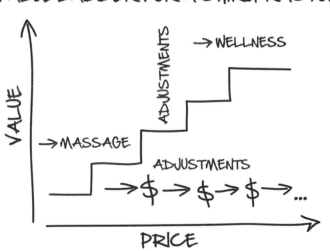

Fig 2.5: Once my friend had a fully developed Value Ladder, his business completely turned around.

You might be selling a book right now on the frontend and have no idea how to build up a backend Value Ladder. Well, what other value can you provide to people? Can you be more hands-on with them? Can you offer more personal attention? Can you provide ancillary services or physical products that enhance your primary offer? My very first information product was a DVD on how to build a potato gun. (And that just goes to show you can sell *anything* online!) But I figured out how to build a Value Ladder by also selling "Do It Yourself" plans and physical potato guns to our customers.

The Value Ladder is the key to building your marketing funnels and mastering everything else I'm going to teach you in this book. This system does not work if all you have is one thing—like a book or an adjustment. You need to be able to build out a full Value Ladder. Most businesses I look at have one or two pieces of the ladder, but they rarely have all four. Once we add in the missing pieces, the business can start to expand dramatically. There's no end to the level of backend services and experiences you can add. If you keep providing more and more value, people will spend more and more money to keep working with you.

I remember paying twenty-five thousand dollars to be a part of the Bill Glazer/Dan Kennedy Titanium Mastermind program. At the time, my highest backend offer was five thousand dollars. Someone in that program asked me, "So, Russell, what do you sell *next* to the people who paid five thousand?" I told him that I didn't have anything else to offer, and he responded, "Russell, that's a five thousand dollar buyer lead— you need to sell them something else!"

Interestingly, later that night the group (yes, the SAME group that had already paid twenty-five thousand to be in the room) was offered a chance to be in the movie *Phenomenon* with Dan Kennedy for an additional thirty thousand. And nine out of eighteen people in our group bought the offer! That was when I realized that there really is no end to your Value Ladder. It's one of the reasons why we created our million-dollar program. Imagine my shock and excitement the first time someone said yes! A percentage of your audience will always want to pay you the premium to get more value.

The only limit to your value offerings is your imagination. Keep thinking of higher and higher levels of service, and you can keep charging more and more money. There's always something else you can offer.

WHAT IF I DON'T HAVE A VALUE LADDER?

Often times, it's hard for companies to figure out how to add more offers to their Value Ladders. Typically, the process is very easy for someone selling information products because that ascension path has already been created and proven in thousands of different information-based companies. But what if you're selling something else? What if you offer physical products, ecommerce, B2B services, or professional services where the path isn't quite as clear? Sometimes it takes a little thought and creativity.

If you already have a product or a service that you sell in the middle of your ladder, what type of "bait" could you create to attract your dream customer? I have a friend who owns a company that makes custom suits for people. He was stuck selling a high-end service but unable to see how to construct a solid Value Ladder (probably because the "front" at the time was two thousand dollars). After a while, my friend tried giving away free cuff links online. He put the offer up, started to advertise, and within days, he had generated hundreds of perfectly qualified leads. He then took those people through an ascension plan to get them to purchase their own custom suits.

Often times, companies have a frontend product but nothing more to sell on the backend. For that, I love to look at what else they could bundle together. Could they offer a coaching program? How about a live event? What other results or value could they give their clients?

I told you earlier that FitLife.tv's core issue was not a traffic or conversion problem. The only real problem was that they had no Value Ladder. Because of that, they couldn't build out a true sales funnel. They brought people into their funnel, but then the relationship ended. People wanted to give them money, but there was no clear path for them to follow. As soon as they added those things into their business, customers naturally started to ascend the ladder, ultimately paying Drew and his team what they were worth.

While it's not always obvious what you can add to the frontend or the backend of your company, I promise that the solutions are there. I also know that if you want to succeed and beat out your competition, you need to have this Value Ladder in place.

Up Next: In the next chapter, we are going to talk about the basics of building out your sales funnel. But please take the time to fill out your own Value Ladder. Again, unless you have a complete Value Ladder, it's impossible to build out an effective sales funnel.

FROM A LADDER TO A FUNNEL

VALUE LADDER V.S. FUNNEL

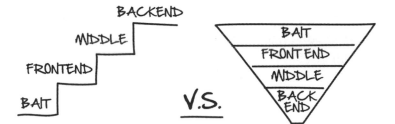

T he Secret Formula was created to help you figure out who you want to serve, how to find them, what kind of bait you should use to attract them, and where you want to take them.

The Value Ladder was created to help you figure out what products and services you need to add so that your dream clients move from your bait to your high-end services.

Now it's time to bridge the gap between a Value Ladder and a sales funnel. In sections 3 and 4 of this book, we will go into a lot of detail about the strategy, psychology, and tactics you need to build out your own sales funnels. But first, I need you to understand what a sales funnel is and how that relates to everything we've discussed so far. This section is short, but critical to your success.

In a perfect world, I would immediately be able to talk my dream client into purchasing my best, most expensive service. But as we discussed in the last chapter, that's almost impossible because I haven't provided value yet. Besides, my highest-level service might not be the best fit for all people. It's almost impossible to build a company just offering your high-end services. You need a full range of offers. So instead of trying to convince someone to buy the most expensive offering right away, we build a funnel that will help us to do two things:

1. Provide value to each customer at the unique level of service that he or she can afford.
2. Make money and be profitable while identifying our dream clients who can afford our highest offer.

The best way to show you how this works is to draw a funnel:

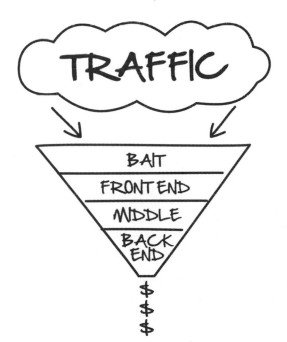

Fig 3.2: A funnel moves people through the sales process.
They enter as prospective customers (traffic), and your job is to
convert as many as possible into repeat customers by selling to
them at the front, middle, and backend of your funnel.

Above the funnel is a cloud that represents all of my potential customers. At the top of my funnel is the "bait" that will attract my dream customers. Notice that this bait is also the first rung of the Value Ladder. As I start to place ads featuring my bait, potential customers will start raising their hands, and a certain percentage of those people will purchase my frontend offer.

Then I will move to the next step in my funnel. Here I will introduce the next product or service in my Value Ladder. This will, of course, be something offering MORE value, while also costing more money. Unfortunately, not everyone who purchases my bait will also purchase this more expensive, high-value product, but a certain percentage of those people will.

From there, I move deeper into the funnel and introduce the next product or service on my Value Ladder. Again, not everyone will buy this product, but a percentage of the clients who initially took the bait will. I will continue to do this through all the levels of my Value Ladder, and at the bottom of this funnel, a handful of people will appear who can afford—and may be willing to purchase—my high-end services. These are my dream clients, the ones I want to work with at a more intimate level.

Now, before I "sell" you on why you need to be thinking about your company in terms of "funnels," I want you to understand that my approach wasn't always this detailed. When I first got started online over a decade ago, there was a lot less competition. I could have just a frontend product, and I'd spend a dollar on ads and make two dollars back in return. But as more people started businesses online and competition started to grow, ad costs went up, the consumer's buying resistance also went up, and it got harder to sell. People I know who were making millions of dollars a year are no longer in business because they didn't adapt and change with the times.

When I started to feel the pinch, I was lucky enough to have some amazing mentors who taught me the importance of building a deeper funnel with more offerings. The deeper your funnel is, and the more things you can offer your clients, the more each customer will be worth to you. And the more they are worth to you, the more you can spend to acquire them. Remember this truth:

"Ultimately, the business that can spend the most to acquire a customer wins."
—Dan Kennedy

Every product I sell online has a sales funnel that I take people through. In fact, immediately after the customer buys something, they are offered an upsell or two before they even leave the page. This is one type of sales funnel. But after they have purchased something from me, I use other types of communication funnels to build a relationship and encourage them to purchase other products and services that we sell. You'll learn about these special communication funnels in Section 2. Every product we sell has its own sales funnel to provide value and convert the buyer into a higher-end customer. You'll see all seven of these funnels in Section 4.

The fact that you picked up this book and are reading it now is proof that this concept works. I already know that a percentage of everyone who buys this book will upgrade to one of my online web classes. I also know that from there, a percentage of those people will upgrade to my Ignite program or my Inner Circle program. And a few, the ones who are the right fit, will join my million-dollar program, and I'll be coming out to set up this whole system in their offices.

Let's Review: So a sales funnel is just the online process you take someone through to get them to ascend through the different levels of your Value Ladder. It's the actual webpages that will make the Secret Formula work. The Secret Formula will help you find your dream customer, offer them your bait, and lead them to where you want them to go—all while providing the customer value and making you money.

Up Next: So, the next logical question, after you understand the concept behind the sales funnel, is WHERE do you find the people to put into that sales funnel? Secret #4 will present three simple questions to help you find your dream clients and bring them to your websites—with credit cards in hand.

HOW TO FIND YOUR DREAM CUSTOMERS

YOUR DREAM CUSTOMERS

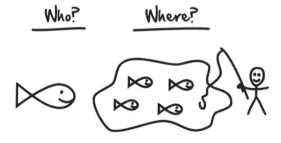

Who?   Where?

With the Secret Formula, you discovered that you must find out *who* your dream clients are and then find out *where* they are. Usually my clients can figure out pretty quickly who they want to sell to, but they get stuck figuring out where those dream clients are and how to get them to visit their websites. The process of getting people to come to your website is called "driving traffic." So when I talk about "traffic" throughout this book, I'm talking about the people you are convincing (through an ad) to come to your website. People always ask me how to attract more traffic to their websites, but before we can address how to get those people, you have to understand the concept of "congregations."

One of the coolest things about the Internet is the power of congregations. These seemingly unimportant groups of people gathering together in little corners of the Internet make it possible for people like you and me to get into business quickly and be successful without all the barriers and expensive hurdles of traditional media.

When I say the word *congregation*, what's the first thing that pops into your head? For most people, the word *congregation* brings to mind a church. A church is really nothing more than a group of people who gather together based on similar beliefs, values, and ideas. For example, each week, the Baptists all congregate together based on their similar beliefs and values. The Catholics also congregate together and so do the Mormons, Seventh Day Adventists, Muslims, and Jews, etc., . . . right? So, if I were selling a perfect product for Mormons, where would I go to sell it? Of course, I would go to the Mormon Church. My dream customers would be right there congregated together. All I'd have to do is put my message out in front of them.

My point is not to teach you how to sell things to churches. I want you to understand the power of a congregation because it's one of the main reasons the Internet is such an amazing tool for businesses. Prior to the Internet, it was hard for people around the world to congregate together. We were limited by location and ability to communicate. But now it's possible for anyone and everyone to congregate together and discuss almost anything with groups of people who hold similar beliefs.

When I was in high school, there were five or six kids who would get together every day at lunch and play card games. I remember one of the games was called Magic: The Gathering. Now I had never heard of it, and I thought the kids were kind of strange sitting by themselves playing cards. But they were content to congregate together and participate in an activity they enjoyed. I'm sure there were a handful of kids in high schools all over the country doing the same thing, unaware of one another. Before the Internet, that was how things worked. You were kind of limited based on geography; you might not be close to other people in your congregation. As a marketer, I would have found it difficult to reach five kids at one high school and three at another school and six or seven at yet another. It would have cost too much money to be successful. Yet now, thanks to the Internet, those five or six kids in my high school can congregate with others all over the world to play Magic: The Gathering online. They can hang out on forums and play games with people half way across the world. Now, if I have a product to sell to a congregation of people who love Magic: The Gathering, it's easy and economical to go online, find where they are, and get my message in front of them.

Here's another example: I was a wrestler in college, and every night all the student athletes had to spend two hours in study hall to make sure we got our homework done. Naturally, I would sit next to my wrestling buddies, and we'd goof off online. I remember looking over one day and noticing that all my friends were looking at the exact same website I was. It was called TheMat.com—a website for wrestlers. We were all chatting about what had happened that month in the world of wrestling and who was winning. We were showing cool moves and discussing what move might work better. Every single person on my college wrestling team was in that study lab for two hours every night hanging out on TheMat.com and talking about wrestling—rather than doing our homework.

Interestingly, this was probably happening in every single university around the country. Add in all the high school wrestlers and any older people interested in the sport who would likely find this site, and you can see that potentially every single wrestler in the world could congregate in one spot and talk about wrestling. Now, if I had a wresting product, what would I do to sell it? I would find the existing congregation of wrestling fans, and I would put my message out in front of them. Simple!

There are congregations for *everything* you can dream up—from antiques buyers to zipper collectors. Once you understand the core concept of congregations, driving traffic is incredibly easy. Not sure where your congregations are? Just go to Google and type in your keywords plus the word *forum* or search for groups related to your keywords on Facebook. It might take a little digging, but you'll find your target audience. Now, there are three questions you have to ask yourself to find and really tap into these congregations.

QUESTION #1: WHO IS YOUR TARGET MARKET?

When I ask that question, people tend to answer with straight demographics like, "My target market is women from ages thirty-six to forty-five who make fifty thousand dollars a year." For a very long time, straight demographics like that were pretty much the only way to separate the people you wanted to target from the rest of humanity. Traditional media catered to certain demographics through its programming and sold advertising along those lines. If you wanted to reach well-off, intellectual men, you might advertise on the late night news or in *The New York Times*. If you wanted to reach housewives, you might advertise during a soap opera in the middle of the day. Unfortunately, straight demographics don't give you any of the juicy information about the individual. In the old days, the best you could do was group people in general terms, according to age, gender, income, and geographical location. The Internet has changed all that. Today you can get as granular as you want to with the data available. You can segment people based on musical taste, medical background, and shoe size. If you like, you can even group according to the movies they watched last month or the websites they visited yesterday.

Because marketers are now able to target so many different characteristics so accurately, people have lost all patience for generalized, mass media messages. Consumers expect and demand that your advertising be *extremely* relevant to them. Say you own a local pet food company and your advertising speaks to women in Tampa who love dogs. If I'm a man in Tampa who loves cats, you might want to create a separate message for me. It doesn't matter that both target markets can get food for their animals at your store. Consumers want and expect messaging that speaks directly to them, or they will likely ignore you. There's just too much information bombarding us at all hours of the day and night. As modern humans, we are subconsciously forced to screen out anything that doesn't directly apply to us. So a dog food commercial may not even register on a cat owner's radar, even though your store also sells cat food.

To create hyper-targeted messages, you have to know your target market inside and out. Successful businesses get inside of the customer's mind and find out what the individual really cares about. What are their pains and passions? What do they desire? What do they think about, and what do they search for online? When you can find out those tiny details, you can search more specifically and find buyers in not-so-obvious places. For example, in the "how to make money" business that I have, I often think back to myself when I was a twelve-year-old kid buying stuff from infomercials. What were my desires? What got me excited? Where did I look for more information? What words and phrases was I searching for? What magazines did I read? I try to figure out what my mindset was at the time. If I had a wrestling product, I would think back to my own wrestling days. Who are the people in the wrestling market? What are they searching for? What problems do they want to solve? What questions do they need answered? I suggest digging into your own experience to create as detailed a picture as possible for the product you are selling. You want to go way beyond typical demographics when answering question number one: Who is your target market? Then, when you have an accurate picture, you can move on to the next question.

QUESTION #2: WHERE IS YOUR TARGET MARKET CONGREGATING?

Remember your target market is made up of real people, so you need to look at their real behavior. Where do they hang out online? Where do they spend their time? What email newsletters might they subscribe to? What blogs do they read? What Facebook groups are they a part of? Are they even on Facebook—or do they prefer Instagram? What keywords are they searching for on Google? What books are they buying on Amazon? Answering these questions can take some time and research, but it's worth taking as much time as you need to develop a clear picture of where your ideal clients are directing their attention.

Finding traffic on the Internet really is as easy as answering these questions. Marketers try to make it complicated with all of the technology that helps direct the traffic to certain web pages. But it's your knowledge of the *people* in your market that makes the technology useful. I like to think of the Internet as a huge mountain, and your ideal customer—your traffic—is gold inside that mountain. Your job as a marketer is to find the gold and mine it out. When you start mining, you're just digging around, poking and prodding, trying to find where the gold is. You know there's gold in that mountain somewhere, but you're not sure where. So you're looking around, trying this area and that area, and all of a sudden, you might dig up a few nuggets. Typically, gold clumps together in a vein running through the mountain (like a congregation). So when you find a little bit of gold, you can dig deeper and find more. You'll soon see that the vein runs deep into the mountain. If you keep following that vein, you can mine out all the gold. It's worth taking the time to do a thorough job in the poking and prodding stage. Because if you can find exactly where your target market is hanging out, then pulling out the gold is simply a matter of putting a relevant message in front of them and directing them to your offer.

Do some digging—all the while asking the crucial questions: *Who is my target market? Where are these people congregating?* You search for a little while, and Boom! You might find an email newsletter they subscribe to. That's a vein of gold. You're going to tap into that. You might buy ads in that newsletter and try to entice all those people back to your website. You might find a blog they frequent or maybe a Facebook group they like. As the entrepreneur, it's your job to go out there and find these congregations. There are people you can hire to help, and there are systems you can set up to tap into those congregations, but first you have to get into the mindset of the target market and figure out where they congregate.

Then you're ready for the third question.

QUESTION #3: HOW CAN YOU GET A CUSTOMER TO LEAVE THE CONGREGATION AND CHECK OUT YOUR PAGE?

If I'm in the middle of a wrestling debate on TheMat.com, it's going to take something special to get me to leave that site and go look at something else. At this point, you have to figure out what offering is special enough to entice a wrestling fan away from his favorite site. How can you divert attention away from what your prospect is currently doing? I call this process the Enquirer Interrupt.

Fig 4.2: Your ads must be able to grab people's attention
if you want them to click over to your site.

Did you know that *The National Enquirer* is one of the most read newspapers in the world? They place their publication in one of the busiest spots on earth: the checkout stand. People only have a split second to make a buying decision, so the publication offers short two- to three- word headlines that will stop almost anyone in their tracks. The magazine is an undisputed master at interrupting your brain patterns and making you notice.

Your job online is almost the same. You are trying to engage someone who is already checking email, Facebook, and his cell phone at the exact same time. You have to interrupt potential customers long enough for them to click on your ad and visit your website.

As you start to think about what type of ads should you be placing—what they should say, what types of images they should use—I recommend going to Google images and searching for "National

Enquirer headlines." You'll see hundreds of examples that you can model. If you look closely, you'll notice the magazine always uses a strange or unusual picture to grab the eye. Then it uses short, punchy headlines (usually describing something weird, unusual, or shocking) to make you curious enough to buy a copy. The images and headlines interrupt whatever you were thinking about to make you pay attention to the product, a magazine.

In our ads, we place these Enquirer Interrupts to grab our prospects' attention and send them to our squeeze pages, our frontend offers, and our bait. Remember that just because you've identified *who* your dream prospects are and *where* they are, your job isn't done. You still need to grab their attention and get them to click over to your website. You do that through these interrupt-style ads.

YOUR ROLE AS THE ENTREPRENEUR

As the entrepreneur for my companies, one of my primary jobs is to identify where the veins of gold are located. This task is not for the person buying the ads, optimizing the ads, or picking the keywords, etc. That's like expecting a building contractor to know how to pour the foundation, frame the house, put up the sheet rock, and run the electricity. A contractor does not need to know how to do all of those things to build a house. In fact, if he did do all of those things, it would take ten times longer to get the job done. Instead, he understands the pieces that need to be in place to build a house, and then he hires the electrician to do the wiring and the sheet rock guy to put up the sheet rock.

Your job as the entrepreneur is to understand the strategy behind these DotComSecrets and then hire the Facebook guy to run Facebook ads and the Google guy to run Google ads. To this day, I've never once run a Google or a Facebook ad, yet I've made millions on both platforms.

I understand the strategy, and then I set up systems and hire people who are great at the tactics. In this way, we all do what we are best at.

Because I know this division of labor works, I'm not going to go into every detail on how to run the ads in this book. Instead, I want to focus on the strategy. Then, you can build a system and have your team help you to implement it. In the next chapter, I'm going to help you understand the strategy behind the three types of traffic, and we will pinpoint your ONLY goal when driving traffic online.

THE THREE TYPES OF TRAFFIC

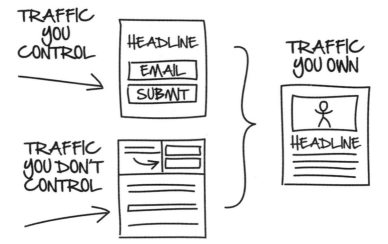

A crucial DotComSecret you must understand to experience exponential growth is this: There are only three types of traffic:

1. Traffic you control PAID TRAFFIC (iE. FACEBOOK Ab)
2. Traffic you don't control SEARCH | SOCIAL MEDIA
3. Traffic you OWN SUBSCRIBERS & BUYERS

Once you understand how each type of traffic works and how they tie together, you will have the ability to direct the right traffic to the right offers, and convert the highest number possible into buyers and repeat clients. Your one and ONLY goal is to OWN all the traffic you can. That is how you grow your list and increase your sales.

TRAFFIC YOU OWN

I want to begin our discussion with the third type of traffic listed above because it's the most important. Traffic you own is the BEST kind of traffic. It's your email list or your followers, readers, customers, etc. I call this the traffic that I "own" because I can send out an email, post a message to my followers, or make a blog post, and I will generate instant traffic. I don't have to buy it from Google or Facebook. I don't have to do any PR or SEO. This is my own distribution channel; I can send out messages anytime I want, with no new marketing costs. I can sell things to these people over and over again, and all of that money comes back as pure profit.

I was lucky when I first got started online to have a mentor named Mark Joyner. Mark had built a huge company online, and when I started to study under him, his number one piece of advice to me was this: "Russell, you have to build a list." He ingrained that principle into my mind, and it became my only focus for two to three years. As my list started to grow, so did my income.

The first month, I was able to get about two hundred people to join my list, and I made just a little over two hundred dollars that month. When I had increased my list to about one thousand people, I started to average about one thousand dollars per month. When I got my list to ten thousand people, I was averaging over ten thousand dollars per month! And those numbers have stayed pretty consistent now that we have well over five hundred thousand people on the lists.

Yes, we average about one dollar per month for each name on our email lists. In some of the markets we're in, the profit is actually a lot higher than that. But as a rule of thumb, when you follow the communication funnels you'll learn in Section 2 correctly, you should expect to see similar results. Once you understand that metric, suddenly list building becomes a much higher priority!

That's why it's so important to convert the other two types of traffic (both traffic you control and traffic you don't control) into subscribers and buyers (traffic that you own) as quickly as possible. The bigger your list, the more money you make.

TRAFFIC YOU CONTROL

The next type of traffic is traffic you control. You control traffic when you have the ability to tell it where to go. For example, if I purchase an ad on Google, I don't own that traffic (Google does), but I can control it by buying an ad and then sending those who click on that ad anywhere I want. Any kind of paid traffic is traffic you control, including the following:

- Email ads (solo ads, banners, links, mentions)
- Pay-per-click ads (Facebook, Google, Yahoo, etc.)
- Banner ads
- Native ads
- Affiliates and joint ventures

Now, I personally LOVE traffic that I can control, but my big problem is that every time I want more of it, I have to spend more money. So my goal is always to send any traffic that I am going to purchase over to a type of website we call a "squeeze page." (We'll discuss squeeze pages a lot more during Secret #11: The Twenty-Three Building Blocks of a Funnel.)

Fig. 5.2: Squeeze pages have one goal, and no distractions.
There is only one thing for the visitor to do on this page.

This squeeze page is a very simple page with ONE goal: to convert traffic that you control into traffic that you own. I send all of my paid traffic to a squeeze page, and when the visitors get there, they only have ONE option: give me an email address or leave. Now a certain percentage of people will leave, but the cool thing is that some of those people will give you a personal email address. After that, the traffic you control becomes traffic that you own, and you can start sending the new potential buyer through your Soap Opera Sequences (Secret #7) and your daily Seinfeld emails (Secret #8).

TRAFFIC YOU DON'T CONTROL

This last type of traffic just shows up, and I don't have any control over where it came from or where it goes. For example, if someone mentions my book on Facebook, their followers may search my name in Google, and they may land on some random page in my blog. I didn't have control over any part of that sequence of events. There are lots of types of traffic that I don't control, including:

- Social media (Facebook, Twitter, Instagram, Google+, LinkedIn, Pinterest, etc.)
- Search traffic (search engine optimization or SEO)
- Guest blog traffic
- YouTube
- Guest interviews

Now, just like traffic that I control, my ONLY goal with traffic that I don't control is also to turn it into traffic that I own. To do this, I try to push all traffic that I don't control back to my blog. If you visit any of my blogs, you'll notice that the top third of my blog is nothing but a glorified squeeze page. When people go there, the only real thing they can do is give me their email addresses. After they do that, they become traffic that I own, and I can put them into my communication funnels.

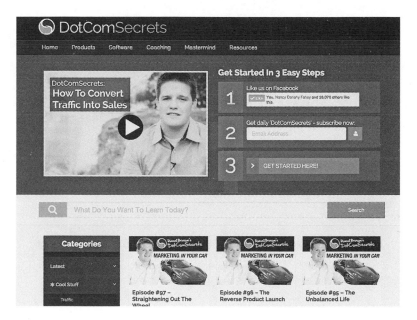

Fig. 5.3: I turn my blog posts into modified squeeze pages
to convert as much traffic as possible into traffic I own.

MOVING INTO YOUR COMMUNICATION FUNNEL

Up Next: Now that you understand where you can find congregations composed of dream clients and you understand that your goal is to convert those people into traffic that you own, the next question is, *What do you do with the potential customers after they join your email list?*

Section 2 of this book will show you how we communicate with our audience. It will detail what emails we send out and in what sequence we send them. It will show you how to use your email list as a tool to get people to ascend your Value Ladder. But before we get into the actual sequences that you'll be sending out (Secret #7 and #8), you first have to understand the Attractive Character.

······················

SECTION TWO:

YOUR COMMUNICATION FUNNEL

······················

SECRET #6:

THE ATTRACTIVE CHARACTER

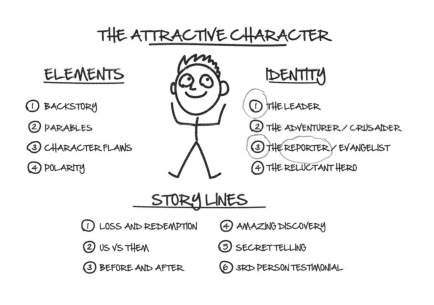

Hey Russell, I'm building a list, but nobody's opening my emails. Nobody's clicking on my links. Nobody's buying what I'm trying to sell. What am I doing wrong?!"

People who started my DotComSecrets course used to express this same thought all the time. Business owners often get behind the idea that they should be averaging a dollar per month for every person on their list. So, they focus on growing their lists, yet feel stuck and frustrated when they don't see results. Can you relate to that at all?

In my experience, the missing link is this concept of the Attractive Character (AC). It's about the persona you're sharing with your audience and how you communicate with your list. Most people either don't bother to create this character, or they don't do it correctly. So, I want to explain the process to you now. It's one of the most important steps you can take when it comes to making sales. Once you intentionally create your AC, your business will change forever.

An Attractive Character is not someone who is extraordinarily good looking, although they might be. What I'm talking about here is a persona that *attracts* clients or customers and helps you build your following to eventually make sales. An Attractive Character allows you to build a platform anywhere you want, whether on email, Facebook, or YouTube. It doesn't matter where you show up; your AC will draw people to you.

The first time I learned about personas and characters, I was at a marketing seminar and heard John Alanis speak. If you look up his name, you'll find he teaches men how to get women to approach them. In other words, he teaches guys how to pick up chicks. I remember he explained how the concept of attracting women was very similar to attracting customers and making sales. If a guy wants a woman to be attracted to him, there are certain things he needs to do. And they are the same things you need to do if you want clients and customers to be attracted to you in your business. He said entrepreneurs need to create an Attractive Character. This was the first time I had ever heard anyone talk about this idea. I listened to him talk for an hour, and it made a huge impact on me and my company.

Think about any business—online or offline. Most successful ones have an Attractive Character front and center. Take Subway, for example. Subway used to be just another fast food restaurant like McDonald's, Burger King, and all the rest. Then somewhere along the line, the company found this guy named Jared. He was a big guy who weighed over four hundred pounds. However, he started eating nothing but Subway twice a day, and over the course of a couple of years, he lost a ton of weight. Subway shared Jared's story with the world. They put him in commercials, on billboards, everywhere. By making Jared their Attractive Character, Subway transformed its business from an average fast food restaurant to a weight-loss plan. This new tactic completely set the company apart from the competition. One of the reasons that Subway does so well is because it focuses marketing tactics around an Attractive Character. People trying to lose weight can relate to Jared. They understand his backstory, and they want to be like him. If this guy could lose all that weight just by eating Subway twice a day, then they can too. This same guy has been bringing in business for Subway for over fifteen years!

Now think about your favorite movies. What was the last movie you saw? Did you see it because you thought the storyline was intriguing? Or did you go because one of your favorite actors or actresses was in it? Movies use Attractive Characters because those ACs bring in the customers. A great example of that concept is the movie *Ocean's Eleven*. When I saw the lineup for that movie, I had no doubt it would be successful. Producers brought in eleven Attractive Characters, actors who viewers already loved, put them together in a movie, and Boom! Instant hit. Maybe you're not a big Brad Pitt fan, but you love everything

Julia Roberts does. So, you go see the movie because she is the Attractive Character you relate to.

This is why sequels and franchises work so well, generation after generation. If you loved Harrison Ford as Han Solo in 1977, you probably paid to see all the *Star Wars* sequels and *Raiders of the Lost Ark*, too. And guess what? Nearly forty years later, guess who's showing up again to bring you a little more Han Solo? It's amazing to think that one mediocre movie created over a generation ago can still pack the theaters and sell tickets by the millions. That's the power of Attractive Characters. We love them. We want to be like them. We relate to their stories. And we buy what they're selling!

This is one of the big secrets behind the most successful online businesses in the most competitive markets, like weight-loss, dating, financial investing, supplements, and ecommerce. All these types of businesses can use an Attractive Character.

I started noticing how this works in my own business when I started speaking at seminars and selling products from the stage. The first few times I spoke, I was still in school at Boise State University. I was a student athlete in the wrestling program, and that information would come out when I told my story from the stage. I talked about wrestling and coaches and lessons I'd learned from the sport. When it was time to sell at the end of the presentation, I noticed that the people who came to the back to buy my product were mostly male athletes. They would say, "Hey, man, I played football in college." Or, "Hey, I'm a lacrosse player." I didn't realize it at the time, but my story was promoting an Attractive Character that other male athletes could relate to. Interesting.

A few years later, my wife and I were trying to start a family. Like so many couples these days, we had some trouble getting pregnant. We went through a long process, but after a few months with a fertility doctor, we ended up getting pregnant with twins. I remember speaking at a seminar, and for some reason, I felt like I should tell that story. I was kind of nervous because I didn't usually share intimate, personal stories. But for whatever reason, I did share that story with the audience and tied it back to my presentation. Then I went through my sales close as usual.

When I looked to the back of the room, something weird happened. The athletes were still there, but now there were wives, mothers, and families buying my products, too. I thought, *How interesting! I shared something about my family, and suddenly there's a new segment of the audience attracted to that part of my persona.* This new audience segment suddenly felt they could relate to me, so they had enough trust to purchase from me. That had never happened before.

I remember another time when my company was launching a product called MicroContinuity. Before we released the product, we had done a few workshops teaching the system to people. One student, Joy Anderson, launched a very successful MicroContinuity program, which is still successful today. When it came time to launch the product, I decided I was tired of telling my story, so I decided to tell Joy's story instead. So, we launched the product and sold over eight thousand units, grossing over a million dollars in sales in just two weeks. A few months later, we had a workshop for people who had bought the program. I remember being amazed as I looked out over the audience and saw a fifty/fifty split of men and women. Typically, my workshops are about 90% men, but this one was totally different. At the end, we surveyed the attendees to find out why they had come to the workshop. Almost without exception, all the women said, "I want to be Joy Anderson."

I kept seeing examples of this trend; the people who related to my stories were the ones who bought my products. So, a few years ago, I started teaching this concept of the Attractive Character. The students who implemented what I'm about to teach you here totally transformed their businesses. All of the major success stories from any of our coaching programs got results by building huge brands and platforms around an Attractive Character.

This concept can mean the difference between making one thousand dollars a month and making one hundred thousand a month. How attractive are you? How interesting are you? Why would someone tune in to watch a TV special about your story? You might be thinking, *But I'm not that interesting.* I promise that I didn't feel very interesting when I first started out either. But if you find ways to share your backstory, you can make it compelling, and people will follow you because of a personal connection.

There are three components to creating an Attractive Character:

- Elements
- Identity
- Storylines

You need each of these components to round out a character people will like and follow. In the upcoming chapters, we will discuss how to introduce the facets of your Attractive Character to your audience, but for now, you need to focus on building out your own Attractive Character profile. We're going to go through that process in detail right now.

THE FOUR ELEMENTS OF THE ATTRACTIVE CHARACTER

1. Backstory. Every good Attractive Character has to have a backstory. It's essential if you want results. If you turned on the TV and saw Jared sitting there eating a sub, what would your reaction be? You'd probably think something like, *Who's that annoying skinny guy just sitting there eating subs all day?* Without knowing his backstory of amazing weight loss, you would be unable to relate to him. He'd just be a dude eating subs.

But if you see Jared's backstory—pictures of him at 425 pounds and 190 pounds—and then see him eating subs, it's a whole different story. You might think, *I'm just like he was. If he can lose all that weight just by eating subs, maybe I can too. I want to be where he is.* Do you see the difference in a potential customer's reaction?

You share your backstory because you want people to see where you came from. If they can relate to where you came from, then they will want to follow you to where you are now. If they don't see the backstory, potential customers won't follow you or listen to you. You'll seem untouchable; you won't seem real to them. However, if they see that you were once in a similar situation, then they instantly identify with you and will follow you. Your story has provided a hook. You can then lay out the path, and they will want to follow that path.

The key is that the story has to relate to the product you're selling somehow. If you're selling a weight-loss product, you want to talk about a weight-loss backstory. If you're selling investing advice, you want a financial backstory. Does that make sense?

Now, if you don't have a backstory that relates to your product, that's okay. You can find someone else's backstory and use that instead. This is what I did when I shared Joy Anderson's story and suddenly became attractive to female buyers. Your students, your case studies, your successful clients—those are all resources for relatable backstories and Attractive Characters. The owner of Subway wasn't the guy on TV eating subs all the time, right? It was Jared. He was the chain's success story, so he became its Attractive Character. Your Attractive Character does not have to be you, but a backstory is essential.

2. Attractive Characters Speak in Parables. Parables are little stories, easy to remember, that illustrate a relevant point. If you've been following me for a while, you know I tell lots of stories, or parables.

For example, when I taught my Expert Secrets course, I needed a way to show people that they can make money with *any* of their talents or skills. So I shared the story, or parable, about the first product I created: a DVD about how to make potato guns. Now, there is a lot to that story that I won't cover here in this book, but it illustrates the fact that you can create and make money selling your experience or expertise in almost anything.

I have other parables that I use to teach the core principles that I want and need my customers to understand. Think about other teachers you've had in the past, those who had a great impact on your life. My guess is that if they had a lasting impact on you, it's because they taught you by using amusing and memorable stories.

A parable is a story about something that happened in your Attractive Character's life. Most people let life pass them by, and they don't stop to take note of the interesting things that happen to them. But you're different. You have the ability to use the things that happen throughout your life to teach and inspire others—as well as sell products.

Here is another example of a parable I use almost every time I sell something. My college wrestling coach's name was Mark Schultz. I had just moved into the dorms and gone to my first practice where I had an awesome time meeting my teammates and the coaches. That night, there was a knock on my door. When I opened it, there stood Coach Schultz. He had brought me a videotape of his own wrestling footage. I thought that was pretty cool, but before he left, he asked me for my wallet. When I gave it to him, he opened it, took all of my money out, and handed me back an empty wallet. I was kind of confused, but too nervous to say anything. He then told me, "Russell, if I gave you that tape for free, you'd never watch it. But because you've paid for it now, you made an investment. Now I know you're going to watch it and learn from it." And he was right. Because I had made that investment, I did watch the tape over and over again, and I became a better wrestler because of it. That's the day I learned the power of investment.

Now, I share that parable almost anytime I'm going to ask somebody to make an investment with me. Because I know the potential customer wants success, but I know they can't have it unless they make that investment. Do you see how sharing a parable, like the one about Coach Shultz, is MORE powerful than just telling someone he needs to make a personal investment?

Look through your life, and I promise that you'll start finding these little parables that can help illustrate important points. You can also draw parables from the lives of others. Just know that when you stop teaching facts and start teaching through parables, your messages will stay with an audience longer.

3. Attractive Characters Share Their Character Flaws. This next element is one that most people really struggle with sharing, but it's one of the most important ones to share because it makes you relatable and real. You need to understand that every believable, three-dimensional Attractive Character has flaws. Think about your favorite characters in movies, books, or TV shows. Every character that you bond with emotionally has flaws, right? One of my favorite examples is Superman. He's the Man of Steel. He's invincible. Nobody can kill him. As a storyline, it's not very exciting. But when you introduce Kryptonite and his concern for the welfare of his family, suddenly he has vulnerabilities and flaws—he becomes an interesting character that people care about.

No one wants to hear about the perfect person—because you can't relate. Yet most of us try to put on a perfect facade for our audiences, thereby alienating the real men and women we are trying to reach. Conversely, as soon as the audience knows you're not perfect, that you have character flaws, then they will start to empathize with you. They'll like you more because you are like them: not perfect.

4. Attractive Characters Harness the Power of Polarity. Another challenge people face when communicating with an audience is trying not to offend anyone. So, instead of being a relatable person, speakers become bland and stay neutral on many topics, only sharing safe things everyone will love.

Here's the problem. While that sounds like the logical thing to do—appeasing everyone—the problem is that being neutral is boring. When an Attractive Character tries to win the votes of everyone, they end up reaching no one.

Instead, Attractive Characters are typically very polarizing. They share their opinions on hard matters, and they stick to their guns—no matter how many people disagree with them. They draw a line in the sand. And when they take a stand for what they believe in, they split the audience into three camps: those who agree with them, those who are neutral, and those who will disagree with them. As you start to create that polarization, it will change your "fair weather fans" into diehard fans who will follow what you say, share your message, and buy from you over and over again.

One of the best examples of this concept is Howard Stern. He's very polarizing. People either love him or they hate him. Yet, as you can see from his following on Sirius radio and his role on *America's Got Talent*, people are listening. Think about the podcasts you listen to. Think about the blogs and books you read. Do the Attractive Characters you have bonded with and follow have a polarizing effect on you? Are there people you still follow and listen to—even though you can't stand them or their messages? It's very interesting that we will spend as much time listening to, talking about, and sharing things from people that we despise as we do treasuring the wisdom from our favorite people. Yet, if any of those characters weren't so polarizing, chances are you wouldn't even know who they were.

Being polarizing is kind of scary sometimes. It is scary knowing that once you start sharing your opinions, there will probably be a group of people who disagree with you and will voice their opinions online. If you search for me online, you're going to find out there are people who love me and people who hate me. That's just the way it is. If you're neutral, no one will hate you, but no one will know who you are either. As soon as you start taking sides on important issues, you'll develop haters, but you'll also develop a group of raving fans. Those raving fans are the people who will buy your products and services.

If nobody's talking about you, then nobody knows who you are. It's time to step out of that neutral space and start sharing your opinions. Bring the things you care about into the open.

IDENTITY OF AN ATTRACTIVE CHARACTER

Your Attractive Character will typically take on one of the following types of identities. You get to pick which one you want to be, and once we go over the choices, the right one will probably jump out at you. When you get your identity together, it's going to shape how you communicate and interact with your audience. _BiZ COACH_

The Leader: The identity of the leader is usually assumed by people whose goal is to lead their audiences from one place to another. Most leaders have a similar backstory to that of their audiences and, therefore, know the hurdles and pitfalls the audience members will likely face on the journey to get ultimate results. Usually the desired result has already been achieved by the leader, and his audience has come looking for help along that same path. I am sure that there are leaders you follow in different aspects of your life, and this may be the role that will be the most comfortable for you when communicating with your audience.

The Adventurer or Crusader: The adventurer is usually someone who is very curious, but he doesn't always have all of the answers. So he sets out on a journey to discover the ultimate truth. He brings back treasures from his journey and shares them with his audience. This identity is very similar to the leader, but instead of leading his audience on a journey to find the result, he is more likely to bring back the answers to give them. _TRADE CONSULTANT_

(PODCASTER)

The Reporter or Evangelist: This identity is often one that people use when they have not yet blazed a trail to share with an audience, but have a desire to. So they put on the hat of the reporter or evangelist and go out to discover the truth. Typically, people who use this identity interview dozens, hundreds, or even thousands of people and share those interviews, and all they've learned along the way, with their audience.

This is the identity I used when I got started. I didn't know a lot about marketing online myself, so I started interviewing people. I became a reporter, just like Larry King or Oprah. Because I started interviewing all these cool people and sharing their stories and lessons, I started building an audience of my own. People kept seeing me with these other high-profile people, and over time, I became associated with them. My status went up because I was constantly in the company of high-status people. The knowledge and credibility I gained from being a reporter naturally evolved into my coaching career. Becoming a reporter is a great way to start a business in a niche you don't know much about.

The Reluctant Hero: This is my personal identity now, and typically the one that I try to share with my audiences. This is the humble hero who doesn't really want the spotlight or any fuss made over his discoveries. But he knows the information or the secrets he has are so important that he must overcome his shyness and share them with the world. There's a moral duty that compels him to share all he knows. Many of you may feel this way naturally. The spotlight is uncomfortable, but you know you need to be there. If that's you, the reluctant hero is the perfect identity for you. Play the part.

Leader, adventurer, reporter, or reluctant hero: You probably identify strongly with one of these four archetypes. Determine which type is a good fit and build out your Attractive Character using the traits for that identity. If you're an adventurer, tell stories of adventure. If you're a leader, tell stories about where you've been and where you are going. If you've chosen the right identity for you, it should be fairly easy to take on that role. If you're struggling to create your AC, perhaps you should take another look at your identity.

ATTRACTIVE CHARACTER STORYLINES

Stories are a great way to communicate with your audience. And there are six basic storylines that businesses use over and over again in emails, sales letters, landing pages, and other communications. We use them because they work. Each one is crafted for a specific purpose. Once you learn how to utilize these storylines, you will see for yourself how powerful they are and want to use them over and over in different ways. Let's go over the basic plot structure of each one.

Loss and Redemption: "I had everything. I was on top of the world. Life was great. Then _____ happened. I had to figure my way out of _____. But it turned out to be a blessing in disguise because I went through _____, and I learned/received _____. Now I _____."

Loss and redemption stories are very powerful because they show the upside of going through hardship or meeting challenges. If you have your own loss and redemption story, great! If not, you can always borrow one from one of your followers or even from the mainstream media or a movie you like.

Us vs. Them: You want to use us vs. them stories to polarize your audience. Remember the power of polarity? Using these types of stories will draw your raving fans even closer and give them a rallying cry against the outsiders. I often call out the "talkers vs. the do-ers" on my list. I want people to make a choice about who they are, because if they're with me, then they will be do-ers, continuing to ascend with me.

Before and After: "First I was _____. Now I'm _____."

These are stories of transformation, and they work great in any market. For example, in the weight-loss market, you might say, "First I was fat. Then I tried Program X. Now I'm skinny." Or, try this with the dating market: "First I was lonely and unattractive. Then I got Program Y. Now, I've got chicks all over me." Here is a transformation for the making-money market: "First I was dirt poor, living in a box under a bridge. Then I tried Product Z. Now, I have a mansion in Beverly Hills."

These stories are pretty self-explanatory and simple to write. In fact, you can often tell the whole story with just pictures. But don't let the simplicity fool you. These stories are powerful motivators, and you should use them often.

Amazing Discovery: "Oh my gosh, you guys . . . wait til you hear about this amazing new thing I just discovered! You're not going to believe it, but I hit it out of the park on my first try! I wasn't sure it would work, but it's amazing. You've got to try it!" These stories are huge for selling webinars and teleseminars because they help people believe that the answer they have been searching for is finally available to them.

Secret Telling: "I've got a secret . . . if you want to find out what it is, you need to do _____." This is my favorite type of storyline. My whole company, DotComSecrets, is built around "secret" storylines. The lure of secrets draws the reader into your funnel and up your Value Ladder.

Third-Person Testimonial: Sharing other people's successes with your products and programs provides powerful social proof. Get as many third-person testimonials from your customers, clients, and students as you can. Then sprinkle them liberally throughout your stories. Or use them as stand-alone stories and case studies.

Let's Review: It's time to get started creating your Attractive Character. When I say "create," I don't mean "make it up." I mean to zero in on a story and personality you or one of your clients has. It's real. Start assembling your identity, your stories, your flaws, and your line in the sand. Most entrepreneurs never think about this vital communication tool. And even if they do, they don't put in the time and effort to do a good job creating a believable persona. Like I said before, creating your Attractive Character can mean the difference between making one thousand dollars a month and one hundred thousand.

Up Next: Now that you understand the strategy behind the Attractive Character, let's shift the focus back to how we can use this tool to communicate with your audience and help them to ascend your Value Ladder naturally.

— NEEDS TESTIMONIALS & CASE STUDIES FOR COST of BIL COACHING.

-TEST VERSION OF THIS w/ LEAD FOLLOWUP FOR COS?.

THE SOAP OPERA SEQUENCE

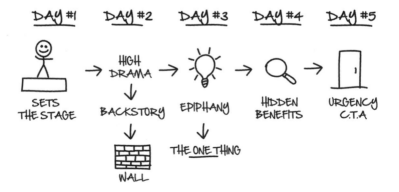

SOAP OPERA SEQUENCE

When somebody joins your list for the first time, it's essential that you quickly build a bond between them and the Attractive Character. The way you introduce your character can mean the difference between a subscriber opening your emails consistently or hitting the delete key. For years I tried dozens of ways to build a quick relationship with people after they joined my list, but I always struggled until I learned a concept called the Soap Opera Sequence from one of my friends, Andre Chaperon.

If you've never watched a soap opera before, the stories rely on open-ended, high-drama episodes that hook the viewers in and keep them coming back every single day to find out what happens next. The programs are continuous narratives that never conclude. The characters are always either getting into trouble or getting out of trouble, falling in love or breaking up, heading to jail or escaping, dying or magically re-appearing. If you relate to the characters, you can't help but get sucked into the drama and want to know what's coming next.

We're going to use the same story structure and elements to create your opening email sequence. The goal is to create an instant bond between your Attractive Character and the person reading the email. If your first email is boring, you're done. They probably won't open the next one. But if you give them something interesting and hook them with an open storyline in the first email, then they will look forward to the next one, and the next, and the next.

In your Soap Opera Sequence, you're going to introduce your Attractive Character and build up an open-ended dramatic story that draws the reader in. There are a few different ways you can do this. For example, I've seen sequences that Andre has built out that have forty or fifty emails! I've never had the time or patience to be able to do that, so instead I built out a simple, five-day Soap Opera Sequence that I send out when someone joins my list. The key to making this sequence work (just like a soap opera) is you have to open and close loops that will drag your reader from one email to the next.

For example, I may tell readers in the first email that I discovered the secret to getting rid of their nerve pain forever without expensive pain medications or side effects . . . but instead of telling them all the details, I merely open that loop and tell them I'll give them the secret tomorrow. Then, in the second email, I will give them the secret, but then I open a new loop that pulls them into email number three.

I'm sure you've seen directors do this on soap operas or reality shows. The tactic pulls you from commercial break to commercial break, from episode to episode. You see it every day on TV; now it's your turn to become a master at it with email.

Let me walk you through the five-email Soap Opera Sequence that readers get when they join my lists. It's simple, and it works to build a relationship with the Attractive Character fast. In this example, someone just joined my list by filling out a form on a squeeze page requesting more information about becoming an "Expert," and the product I'm going to be selling them in this series is called "Expert Secrets."

Email #1: Set the Stage. This is the first email, a thank you note, that people receive the minute they sign up for your list. It sets the stage for the emails to come and lets people know what to expect. Are you going to email them once a day, twice a day, or once a week? For this first sequence, I recommend once a day for the best results.

Here's an Example:

Subject: [DCS] Ch. 1 of 5

Body: Hey, this is Russell, and I want to "officially" welcome you to my world.

About ten years ago, I started my first online business while I was in college (selling potato gun DVDs), and this little hobby became my obsession.

I started selling all sorts of things online and have become a student of marketing.

My other businesses are where I test and try stuff out . . .

DotComSecrets is where I share what I've learned.

My goal is always to give away better stuff for FREE than what other people charge for.

In fact, tomorrow I'm gonna do just that. Yes, I'm going to let you go through one of my BEST products for free—and then ONLY pay me if you think it's worth it . . . BUT only if you open the email when it comes . . .

Yes, you heard me right . . .

I want our relationship to start out great . . .

So, I'm going to WOW you with SO much value that you'll feel obligated to buy stuff from me in the future (just kidding . . . kinda).

Sound good?

Cool, then look for that email tomorrow.

Thanks,

Russell "Your New Marketing Buddy" Brunson

P.S. The subject line is "[DCS] Ch. 2 of 5: The day my education failed me" —so look for it!

Email #2: Open with High Drama. Okay, if you did a good job opening a loop in email number one, then the reader will be anxiously waiting for your next email to come in. For me, this is where the story "selling" process begins. I learned from Daegan Smith that you ALWAYS start any good story at the point of high drama. Most people mistakenly start their stories at the beginning, but usually stories don't get good until the middle, so it's better to start at the good part, and then you can go back and fill in the backstory after readers are hooked.

Backstory. Once you have their attention with emotional drama, you're going to go back and tell them the backstory. Tell them the events that led up to the high-drama moment. How in the world did you get yourself into such a predicament? Typically, your backstory is going to take you back to a similar spot the readers may be in now. If you're helping them to lose weight, you take them back to when you were overweight. If you're teaching them finances, take them back to a time before you were successful. You want to bring them on a personal journey with you.

This backstory will lead up to a spot where you got stuck and hit a wall. Usually this is where the readers are in their lives right now. They are stuck, and that is why they are open to your answers. You explain to them how you hit that wall and then found the answer. But don't give them the answer yet. Just open the loop, and promise to close it in email number three.

Here's an Example:

Subject: [DCS] Ch. 2 of 5: The day my education failed me.

Body: "How did I get here?"

I sat in the middle of a full auditorium, feeling a little confused that after everything, it would all end here . . . like this.

I had been blindly following the status quo for fifteen years, moving towards one goal, only to find out the whole thing was a lie . . .

I looked to my left . . . and I looked to my right . . . and I saw hundreds of others in the same situation as me. Only THEY had smiles on their faces.

Didn't they know what was about to happen to us?

It was Saturday, May 14th, 2005.

It was the day I was finally graduating from college, the day my parents had told me about for years.

"You need to get a college education so you can get a good job."

Sure, tonight there would be a lot of celebrating . . .

But what about the next morning?

That's when we all had a chance to meet the "Real World."

And as we quickly found out, it's not very nice or forgiving.

For most of the people who graduated with me, IF they were able to find jobs, they were going into entry-level jobs making thirty to forty thousand dollars a year . . .

Barely enough to cover the monthly payments for their student loans.

Loans which, by the way, are non-dismissible . . . EVEN if you declare bankruptcy.

The chains of debt and a job market that can't pay enough to cover the costs of our education is what we each inherited when we stepped into the "Real World."

So, when I looked around and saw them all smiling on graduation day, at first I was confused . . .

Not for me, but for them . . .

Because for me, I knew what my next step was. Just two years earlier, I had stumbled on a cool way to take the things I was good at in my life and turn those things into a business.

This was a business that had made me two hundred and fifty thousand dollars my senior year in college and would go on to make me over a MILLION dollars within just one year of graduation.

Would you like to know what I found out? Are you interested in how I was able to get my idea up and running with literally no money, while I was going to school, wrestling, and spending time with my new wife?

If so, then look for my email tomorrow. I'm gonna show you the epiphany I had, but more importantly, I'm going to explain how you can use it to get similar results in your life!

So, look for tomorrow's email. The subject line is [DCS] Ch. 3 of 5: Expert Secrets.

Thanks,

Russell "Wish I Had My Tuition Back" Brunson

P.S. I almost forgot. I told you yesterday that I was going to GIVE you my best product for free . . .

You can get it here (but please don't share it with anyone else)—this is for my faithful subscribers only:

www.ExpertSecrets.com/freeaccess <= my best product

This course has made more of my students independently wealthy than anything we've ever done in the past. So go signup for the training now and let's see where it could take you!

Talk to you tomorrow!

Email #3: Epiphany. Now it's time to start bringing in the dawn. You have an epiphany. You realize something you hadn't thought of before. Maybe it's something that was right in front of you the whole time. It's the moment that everything turned around for you. By now the reader is so hooked in, they want to know (and hopefully buy) your solution. Most of the time, your epiphany email will lead back to your core offer—whatever you're selling that solves the problem.

- My epiphany was I needed to build a list, and that's when I learned about _____.
- I had to get a support system to help me get over my addiction; that's when I found _____.
- I had to address the emotional roots of overeating, and that's when I discovered _____.

The epiphany ties into the solution you're selling. If you're selling someone else's product, it's enough to say your epiphany led to the discovery of the product.

Here's an Example:

Subject: [DCS] Ch. 3 of 5: Expert Secrets.

Body: I was sitting in my college classroom, doing the math and trying to figure out how much my college professor was making per hour.

I assumed he was making about fifty thousand dollars per year. (My estimate may have been low or high; I have no idea.) If he was working forty-hour weeks, then he was probably making about twenty-five dollars an hour.

I then looked at a "how to" book I had bought the night before. I had paid fifty dollars for the book, and I thought it was awesome.

I knew the person who wrote the book had said that he sells, on average, one hundred copies of that book per day. One hundred copies!

I was doing the math, and at fifty dollars per book, he was making about five thousand dollars per day! Or $1,825,000 per year!

But the craziest part is the guy only spent a few days writing the book (it was 90% pictures and just 10% text), and when he was done, he NEVER had to write it again. The book did the teaching for him! He was able to create it once and then get paid for it over and over again!

That's when I realized I didn't want to sell my knowledge by the hour like my professor was doing . . . I wanted to sell it like this author!

And so that's what I did . . .

And by my senior year in college, I had made about two hundred and fifty thousand dollars!

And within a year of graduation, I had made over a million!

And I did this all by focusing on ONE thing . . .

Selling my knowledge the right way!

Would you like to know how I did that?

If so, I just posted a video online that will show you how I took twenty dollars and a simple idea and turned it into a million-dollar-a-year "how-to" business.

I posted the video here: www.ExpertSecrets.com/freeaccess

Go check it out, and let me know what you think.

Thanks,

Russell Brunson

P.S. Tomorrow I want to show you a few hidden benefits that being an "expert" will give you, benefits you probably don't even know exist. Look for that email tomorrow!

Email #4: Hidden Benefits. In this email, you want to point out benefits the reader is getting by knowing you and following your plan or by using your product. You want to focus on benefits that probably aren't as obvious. This gives you another reason to email them, and it gives the prospect another chance to build an even stronger bond with the Attractive Character. This email will point out the hidden benefits they may not have thought about before.

Sure, you're going to make more money—but you also get more freedom to travel.

Sure, you're going to lose weight—but you'll also live long enough to enjoy your grandchildren.

Sure, you're going to be able to work from home—but did you realize you'll be able to take vacations whenever you want?

Often, it's the hidden benefits that really grab the reader and move them to take action. So, you want to come up with parables (stories) that demonstrate those hidden benefits. Show them how you can take time off whenever you want, and explain how that makes you feel. When the reader thinks, *Man, I want that for myself!* That's when they click the link and buy your products.

Here's an Example:

Subject: [DCS] Ch. 4 of 5: The Hidden Benefits.

Body: When I first became an "Expert", I was concerned because I didn't have any credentials, degrees or anything. . .

I just knew that what I showed people worked and I wanted to share it.

But what caught me off-guard was how helping people get what they want in life actually changed the quality of my own life.

Sure, I started to make a lot of money, BUT. . . more importantly, each person I helped opened up new doors for me. Through my "Expert" business, I've been able to travel around the world and meet cool people like Tony Robbins and Richard Branson...

But the REAL hidden benefit has been the fulfillment I get when I see someone else change his or her life. And that is what this business really is about for me, I'm guessing if you're here, then it's probably the same thing for you too—am I right?

If so, then you NEED to signup for my Expert Secrets course. Normally I charge $3,000 to attend, but I am going to do two cool things for you:

I'm giving you a HUGE 90% discount

You're ONLY gonna pay if you like it!

Yes, that's right—you get to come signup, attend, get all of my best ideas—and then IF (and only if) you love it, will you pay.

And if you don't like it for any reason—then you're getting it for free.

Does that sound more than fair?

Cool—then go get your ticket for our upcoming event (it's happening this Thursday) here:

www.ExpertSecrets.com/freeaccess

Thanks,

Russell Brunson

Email #5: Urgency and CTA. This is usually the last email in my Soap Opera Sequence. It's NOT the last email I send people, it's just the end of my introduction. The goal is to give the reader one last push to go take action right now. You do that by adding urgency into the equation and then using a call to action (CTA). Up to now, you've been casually using CTAs, but in this last email, you want to light a little fire under readers. What legitimate reasons can you come up with that would make them need to take action right away?

- Your webinar starts tomorrow.
- You only have ten seats left at your event.
- You only ordered one thousand books, and most of them are gone.
- You're pulling the video offline.

Whatever the reason, it needs to be real. Fake urgency will backfire on you, and you'll lose all credibility. Just think of a reason why you might "run out" of whatever you're selling. If it's an evergreen product, then create a special sale that ends soon. Or give readers a coupon that expires in twenty-four hours. Be creative! There's always some way to create real urgency.

Here's an Example:

Subject: [DCS] Ch. 5 of 5: Last Call.

Body: I've been talking about my "Expert Secrets" class this week, and how you can get a ticket for free. . .

But that special offer is going away TODAY. . .

Yes, if you read this email tomorrow, then I apologize, because it will be too late. If you take this class later, you'll have to pay

AT LEAST $300, but I might put it back to its full ticket price of $3,000 by then as well (haven't decided yet).

But—if you want to take me up on my "try before you buy" offer, and go through the entire 5 ½ hour training BEFORE you spend a dime. . .

Then go get your ticket ASAP here:

www.ExpertSecrets.com/freeaccess

You've been warned – I don't want any emails tomorrow saying I didn't warn you. ☺

So, go get your ticket, and I'll see you on the training.

Thanks,

Russell Brunson

THAT'S HOW THE SOAP OPERA SEQUENCE WORKS:

Email #1 pulls the reader to Email #2 . . .

Email #2 pulls the reader to Email #3 . . .

And so on.

The emails themselves should be easy to read and fast to scan. So, use one or two sentences per line. Add in lots of white space. Do not use long paragraphs that slow people down. I like to write out the basic structure elements first. Then I fill in the juicy details and emotional hooks.

You probably noticed a couple of other things in the example emails. First, I use loads of personality. This is the reader's introduction to my Attractive Character; I want people to bond with me and be entertained. I don't try to hide who I am. And along those same lines, you may have noticed some grammatical errors. Why didn't I fix them? Remember, your Attractive Character needs flaws so people can relate. That goes for your emails, too. I'm not telling you to put errors in on purpose, but if they happen, don't freak out. And please don't let fear of making a mistake keep you from sending out the emails at all.

If you follow the Soap Opera Sequence style, you're going to be amazed by how much more successful you are—early on and as long as you continue to send emails to your list. To make it easy for you to get the hang of this, I've created a special Soap Opera Email Template you can download and use over and over again. By using this template, you'll never forget any of the major elements, and you'll save a ton of time when writing emails.

To download: Go to www.DotComSecretsBook.com/resources/soaptemplates

Up Next: So, you've got your Soap Opera Sequence set up. Now what? How should your Attractive Character communicate with your list going forward?

I'm glad you asked! You're going to use what I call Seinfeld emails. That's the next secret!

SECRET #8:

DAILY SEINFELD SEQUENCE

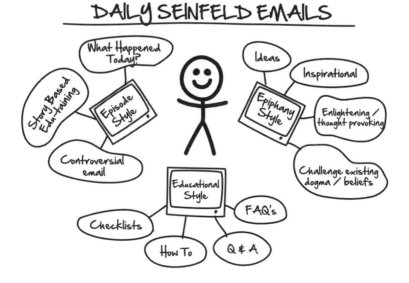

RUSSELL (an NBC executive): So, what have you two come up with?

JERRY: Well, we've thought about this in a variety of ways. But the basic idea is I will play myself.

GEORGE: (Interrupting) May I?

JERRY: Go ahead.

GEORGE: I think I can sum up the show for you with one word: NOTHING.

RUSSELL: Nothing?

GEORGE: (Smiling) Nothing.

RUSSELL: (Unimpressed) What does that mean?

GEORGE: The show is about nothing.

JERRY: (To George) Well, it's not about nothing.

GEORGE: (To Jerry) No, it's about nothing.

JERRY: Well, maybe in philosophy. But, even nothing is something.

(Jerry and George glare at each other. The receptionist enters.)

SUSAN: What's the premise?

JERRY: Well, as I was saying, I would play myself, and as a comedian living in New York, I have a friend, a neighbor, and an ex-girlfriend, which is all true.

GEORGE: Yeah, but nothing happens on the show. You see, it's just like life. You know, you eat; you go shopping; you read . . . You eat; you read. You go shopping.

RUSSELL: You read? You read on the show?

JERRY: Well, I don't know about the reading. We didn't discuss the reading.

RUSSELL: All right, tell me. Tell me about the stories. What kind of stories?

GEORGE: Oh, no. No stories.

RUSSELL: No stories? So, what is it?

GEORGE: (Showing an example) What'd you do today?

RUSSELL: I got up and came to work.

GEORGE: There's a show. That's a show.

RUSSELL: (Confused) How is that a show?

JERRY: Well, uh, maybe something happens on the way to work.

GEORGE: No, no, no. Nothing happens.

JERRY: Well, something happens.

RUSSELL: Well, why am I watching it?

GEORGE: Because it's on TV.

RUSSELL: (Threatening) Not yet.

GEORGE: Okay, uh, look, if you want to just keep on doing the same old thing, then maybe this idea is not for you. I, for one, am not going to compromise my artistic integrity. And I'll tell you something else. This is the show, and we're not going to change it. (To Jerry) Right?

Yes, that was the dialog from one of my all-time favorite TV shows, *Seinfeld*. This was the episode when George and Jerry were trying to pitch their idea to NBC about starting a show about nothing. It was funny because the show *Seinfeld* actually was a show about nothing.

When I first started growing my list, I really struggled to send emails. What did I have to say that was important enough that people would want to open and read it? So I started focusing on writing great, content-packed emails that often took days to write. I thought that was the answer. But I later discovered that after someone had gone through my Soap Opera Sequence and bonded with the Attractive Character, content wasn't what they responded to. What the readers responded to was . . . well, nothing. ☺

My emails switched from 100% content to 90% entertainment and just 10% content, and my readership, opens, clicks, and sales all skyrocketed with the change.

You want your Attractive Character to be fun and entertaining. That's how you're going to write your daily Seinfeld emails. That's right;

I recommend sending them *daily* after your initial Soap Opera Sequence is finished.

I know a LOT of people get VERY nervous about how often they email their lists. I used to feel that way, too. I used to email once a month, and my response rates were horrible. So then I started emailing twice a month. And guess what? I more than doubled my income.

Then I decided to email once a week, then twice, then every other day, and what I've found now is that if I don't email my list every day, I lose money every day. I strongly recommend emailing every day, and if you do it with the "Seinfeld style" I'm going to show you now, readers won't get annoyed because they will be so entertained.

The secret to keeping your subscribers happy to hear from you every day is using the Seinfeld format. Be entertaining. Just talk about your day.

- What's going on in your Attractive Character's life?
- What happened that's embarrassing?
- How are you getting through the holiday season?
- Where are you planning your vacation this year?
- What did you buy recently that you regret?
- What did you buy recently that you just adore?
- What made you scream with rage yesterday, that you're laughing about today?
- What crazy antics did your kid or your dog get into yesterday?
- What funny thing happened in your past that teaches a lesson?

These are emails about nothing. Just random episodes and entertaining stories.

EXCEPT . . . they have a purpose. The goal is to lead people back to whatever you're selling. It might be your core offer or some other product or service. It might even be someone else's product. Every story needs to relate back to something you're selling.

That's the secret. That's how you make money.

If you just send out entertaining emails and don't tie in your products or services, you won't make a dime. Not even if you're the best storyteller in the world. EVERY EMAIL and each story must be tied back into some type of offer for your audience.

Let me show you an example of some Seinfeld emails and how I tie the story back into the product I'm selling. Both these examples made over one hundred thousand dollars each when they were sent out to my list. They are both great examples of emails about nothing.

EXAMPLE #1

Subject: [True Story] He FLUSHED $20 million down the toilet today

Body: So, yesterday we had a guy apply for my Ignite program . . .

I saw his app come through, and I was actually really excited, because he is in the golf market.

Now, I'm no golfer, but I've got a lot of friends doing $20 million + in the golf market online.

I saw his product and KNEW it was a home run.

So, the coach who was going to call him back asked me for my opinion on his business before she called him, and I sat down for ten minutes and pulled up the following:

His three major competitors

Every site competitors were SUCCESSFULLY buying traffic from

The top three converting ads for each of his competitors

The sales funnels that WERE converting and the main reason his was NOT

I then showed her the two media buyers I would use if I were in the golf market (both can send over one thousand sales a day, consistently).

Armed with this information, she called the guy up . . .

He was a little cocky (and rightfully so—he'd sold over 100,000 units of his product on TV). Yet, for some reason, he couldn't figure out this pesky Internet thing . . .

She started sharing some of my ideas with him, and then he stopped her . . .

"Look, I've read twenty books on Internet marketing . . . there isn't a single thing Russell could teach me that I don't already know . . ."

So she tried to explain, "Look . . . you could read a million books on Jiu Jitsu, but that's not gonna help you in a street fight . . ."

I thought that was pretty funny, but what happened next was just sad.

He said, "Well, Russell doesn't know anything about golf . . ." and then he hung up.

Now, while he was right about me not knowing anything about golf . . .

I know EVERYTHING about SELLING golf stuff online.

I've been doing this for OVER ten years now. I've personally trained over 2,500 companies in my office here in Boise.

I've worked with a LOT of golf guys . . . (and one golf gal).

I've worked with people in just about every market I can think of (except bowling . . . I've never had someone teaching bowling come to me, which makes me sad, because bowling is my third favorite sport after wrestling and Jiu Jitsu).

Anyways . . .

For about everything else I can think of, I've mapped out a funnel, shown the client what they were doing wrong, introduced them to my media buyers, advised them on which sites to buy ads from, and instructed them on what they should be spending to acquire a customer in THEIR specific market.

I then usually introduce the client to the gurus I know in those areas. After speaking on Dan Kennedy's stage for six years, I have met most of the "gurus" in most industries, and my position makes it easy to find connections for others.

Those are the things you CAN'T learn in a book . . .

Those are the things we bring to the table for our Ignite people.

My goal for that group is not to teach them more stuff . . . it's to make them more money.

Anyway, if you've got a golf product, let me know, because I've got a killer twenty- million-dollar-a-year blueprint that this dude just flushed down the toilet because of his arrogance . . . or ignorance. Either way, he lost out.

You can just plug in and run with it . . .

Or if you sell, well, almost anything else, I'd love to help with that, too.

Our next Ignite meeting is here in Boise in May. If you'd like to come, you've got to act fast.

You can apply here:

http://Ignite.DotComSecrets.com

Oh, and we only accept cool people. If you like to flush money down the toilet . . . PLEASE don't apply.

Thanks,

Russell Brunson

EXAMPLE #2

Subject: Jiu Jitsu is like wrestling for old, fat guys (and other marketing stuff)

Body: So, tomorrow I'm fighting in a Jiu Jitsu tournament.

For those of you on my list who don't know what Jiu Jitsu is, it's kinda like wrestling for old, fat guys (which is GREAT for me because, while I still look like I'm thirteen, I am actually getting a lot older—34 yrs old now—and fatter—30 lbs. heavier than when I was wrestling).

Anyway, I have weigh-ins in a few hours, and as of right now, **I'm still seven pounds overweight . . .**

Good thing I'm a wrestler and have some awesome weight-cutting skillz. In fact, I just found my old weight-cutting clothes this morning. Check them out:

Yes, they are a little tight, but my three-year-old told me I look like a ninja, so they can't be that bad . . . right?

Anyway, in about an hour, I'm gonna go to the wrestling room, and within thirty to forty minutes, I'll lose all 7 lbs. Then tomorrow, I get to step onto a mat with a bunch of younger, faster guys whose

ONLY goal in life is to choke me out . . . (or to break my arm, whichever comes first).

I'm SO SO SO SO SO SO excited!

So, why do I tell you this?

Because this week, we did well over six figures in sales.

Not this month . . . **this WEEK.**

And we did it WITHOUT any product launches . . .

WITHOUT any affiliates . . .

And while that is a pretty normal week for us, this week was special because we also did it . . .

WITHOUT me actually being in the office . . .

Yup . . .

You guessed it . . . I spent most of this week in the wrestling room, getting ready for the tournament this weekend.

Yet, we still did six figures in sales while I was gone.

Would you like to learn how I did it?

Would you like to see how you build a business that can run just as well when you're gone as when you're there?

Are you ready to take your company to the next level?

If so, I've got good news for you . . .

As long as I don't end up in the hospital after my match this weekend, I'm gonna be coming into the office next week.

That gives me time to work personally with two more people to help build out their funnels . . . (the SAME type of funnel we use to pull in six figures a week like clockwork).

If you're ready to take your game to the next level and create a business that can truly give you time and freedom to do other things you love, then let's get on the phone and figure out how we can work together.

Sound good? If so, then you can apply here:

http://Ignite.DotComSecrets.com

Oh, and if you're looking for a "get rich quick" scheme, this isn't it.

If you're looking for a "**work hard and build an awesome company**" scheme, then I'm your man!

Okay, I'm off to cut weight . . .

Wish me luck this weekend!

Thanks,

Russell Brunson

P.S. I already know that it's not healthy to cut seven pounds in under an hour . . . so no emailing me telling me it's not healthy.

I'm pretty sure that stepping onto a mat with someone 30 lbs. heavier is a lot less healthy than me losing 7 lbs. of water in an hour. Ha ha . . .

Do You See How Seinfeld Emails Work? Do you see how the story eventually ties into a product?

That's how your Attractive Character is going to communicate with your list in every email you send after your Soap Opera Sequence. It's fun. And once you get the hang of it, the writing goes pretty fast. You can even dictate the email, record it on your phone, and then send it to your assistant to be transcribed.

One thing I should note here. These are broadcast emails, not auto-responders.

Soap Opera Sequence emails are set up to be an auto-responder sequence. That means after someone signs up, they get email one on the first day, then email two on the next, etc.

Seinfeld emails are different. After someone has completed your SOAP series, they should be moved to a broadcast list where they will only get the Seinfeld email that you send out that day. Seinfeld emails are typically not lined up in a sequence that everyone has to go through. That doesn't mean you can't write them ahead of time and schedule the broadcasts in your email provider, but typically they are tied to relevant things happening in the life of the Attractive Character as they are happening.

Lastly, these emails do double duty when you put them on your blog. People often ask me what they should write about on their blogs, and I always tell them simply to copy and paste their daily Seinfeld email. It's quick, easy, and consistent blog content that leads people to a sale.

Let's Review: Your Soap Opera (auto-responder) Sequence is your Attractive Character's introduction to your new subscriber. If you follow the outline I provided, you'll notice an increase in your sales simply because people can relate to your backstory and epiphany after they read about it.

Seinfeld emails continue the conversation on a daily basis. The goal is to be fun and entertaining while you sell stuff.

You can get started with this right now. Go download your Soap Opera Sequence template, and write your first five emails.

Then start writing your Seinfeld emails and loading them into your email provider. If you get stuck for ideas, my team has compiled a list of writing prompts for you. Download them at www.DotComSecretsBook.com/resources/seinfeld.

Up Next: Now that you have seen how we communicate with the traffic that we are bringing into our funnels, it's time to shift focus back to building your sales funnel. Section 3 is called Funnelology and will discuss the strategies behind building your successful sales funnels.

················

SECTION THREE:
FUNNELOLOGY
LEADING YOUR CUSTOMERS
TO THE SALE
(OVER AND OVER AGAIN)

················

REVERSE ENGINEERING A SUCCESSFUL FUNNEL

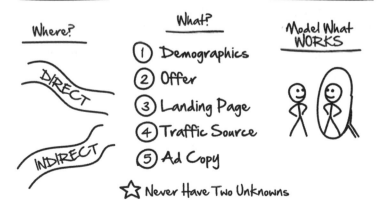

EXISTING TRAFFIC STREAMS

Where?

What?

Model What WORKS

DIRECT

INDIRECT

① Demographics
② Offer
③ Landing Page
④ Traffic Source
⑤ Ad Copy

☆ Never Have Two Unknowns

Before I start to build out any new sales funnel, the first thing I want to do is find other people who already have a successful funnel and are selling to my target market. If I can't find other businesses, then I won't continue to move forward. But if I *can* find others who are already successfully selling to the chosen market, then I can reverse engineer what they're doing and figure out where they are getting their traffic.

The Internet is full of gurus teaching hundreds of different ways to generate traffic, and it seems like a new tactic or trick pops up every day. For me, I focus on one real strategy. I prefer to find out where the traffic already exists and then just plunk myself down in front of it and send it on a little detour to my site. Why work hard to generate traffic when it's already out there waiting for you? This chapter is going to show you how to reverse engineer your competitors' sales funnels. You will learn how to understand what they are doing, where their traffic is coming from, and how to transform their traffic into *your* traffic.

FIVE VARIABLES OF SUCCESSFUL CAMPAIGNS

The first step to reverse engineering existing traffic streams is understanding the five elements that go into any successful online ad campaign. I never start creating a funnel unless I know at least four of these five things. I never want two unknowns. Also, as I'm analyzing my own funnels—if something isn't working—it usually comes down to one of these five things:

1. Demographics
2. Offer
3. Landing page
4. Traffic source
5. Ad copy

Let's look at each variable individually so you can get a clearer picture of what I'm talking about.

1. Demographics. The demographics are all the characteristics of the people you're targeting. The demographics define who belongs in the target group and who doesn't. We're talking about distinguishing factors, like age, sex, education, geographical location, income level, race, language, and political affiliations—any and all characteristics you can think of that define those people you want to reach with your message. For example, our supplement company has an older demographic of men and women. Our coaching company's main demographic is entrepreneurs making between one and three million dollars a year.

If I put the right offer in front of the wrong demographic, it's going to bomb. If I put a wrestling supplement offer in front of older people with diabetes, they're not going to buy. So, we need to make sure we get our demographics right. Once you know the demographics of the people your competitors are going after, it's very simple to know what yours should be.

When I first started working with our pain supplement, I had no idea who to target or where to find the traffic. So my team and I went through this process of reverse engineering some supplements similar to ours, and we found out very quickly where our competitors were placing their ads. We found that some of their ads were on diabetic websites (a segment we didn't know would benefit from our supplement). We found ads running successfully on survival websites, natural health websites, and more. By digging deeper and researching our competitors, a whole new world of opportunity opened for us. After we found some of these new demographics, over the course of two months, we were easily able to scale a product that was making twenty thousand dollars a month to making over five hundred thousand a month now. Pretty cool, huh?

When you know your demographics, you know who your target market is and where they are likely to be hanging out online. You know what sites they're on and where they get together to talk to each other. Once you have that information, it becomes very easy to scale your offer and build your business quickly.

2. Offer. The offer comes down to what you are selling and at what price point you are selling it, including your upsells and downsells. When I want to find out what my successful competitors are offering, I buy their products. Remember, the first offer you see probably isn't the primary offer. It's more likely to be what gets people in the door, while the real moneymakers are down the line somewhere. The first offer is just the tip of the iceberg, and I need to see their ENTIRE iceberg during this research phase.

When I'm researching competitors, I go in and purchase everything they offer me. I will easily spend hundreds of dollars to study their offers and their funnels. And I keep careful notes. This is critical competitive research. I want to know exactly what they're selling, how they're selling it, and at what point they're offering each product in their funnel. What's the copy on the sales videos? What emails am I getting? How many? Are they selling in every email or offering content in some? The more I know, the better chance of success I will have.

3. Landing Page. This is the page a person lands on right after they click on an ad, and I believe it's the most important page in your entire sales funnel. What does that page look like for your successful competitors? Is it an opt-in page? Is it a sales page? What's working for people right now? I'm not going to make up my own landing page and hope it works. I'm going to reverse engineer what's *already working* and model that for my own page. I'm going to make something very similar to what's already successful.

It always comes back to modeling what's already working. It amazes me how so many people put up random sites they think look good, without first investigating successful sites in their niche. Then they wonder why they're not making any money. It's because they're not following a proven model.

I remember when I first heard Tony Robbins speak, and he emphasized that if you want to be successful in any part of your life, you needed to find someone else who is already doing what you want to do and model your efforts after theirs. Nowhere is that idea truer than when you're building a new sales funnel. You need to model what is working. Do NOT try to re-invent the wheel. That's the secret. That's how you take a decade of hard work and compress it down into a day's worth of time and effort. Find what someone else has already done and model it. Start there, and then you can tweak your funnel, test it, and try to improve on that model after you're already making money.

4. Traffic Source. Where is your competitor's traffic coming from? What are the specific websites that competitor buys ads on? Is the traffic coming from banner ads or social media or email? Does he use mainly video or text?

Do not think that you need to "create" traffic. The traffic is already out there. All you have to do is find it, tap into it, and redirect it back to your offer. In just a minute, I'm going to show you some cool tools and techniques you can use to find out exactly where a competitor's traffic is coming from so it's easy to funnel those people to your offers.

5. Ad Copy. This is the last element of a successful campaign. What do successful ads look like? What makes people click on the ad? What's enticing them to even look at the competitor's ad in the first place? What pictures are competitors using? What does the headline say? What does the body copy look like? Are the competitors using video? All these things influence whether a person clicks on an ad or not. Remember, traffic is made up of real people. People can be persuaded to click, but it can take months or years of trial and error to discover how to make that happen. Don't waste time trying to figure it out by blindly tweaking and adjusting your own advertising methods. Find what's already working, and model it. Then once you've got a predictable, steady income, you can run split tests and try to improve on the ad yourself.

The whole reverse engineering process depends upon finding out about all five of these elements in regards to your competitors. Unfortunately, you're not always going to be able to do that. I've gotten really good at the reverse engineering process, but there are still times when I can't find all the banner ads, or I'm not sure about all the demographics. One unknown is not good, but you can usually try to guess and get close enough. If there are two unknowns, I'm probably not going into that market. I want as much data as possible before I start building out my offers, landing pages, and ads. Never move forward with two unknowns. Keep digging, keep researching until you find a niche where you can find all the data you need to move ahead and be profitable.

HOW TO REVERSE ENGINEER A SUCCESSFUL CAMPAIGN

Now that you know what to look for in your competitors' campaigns, I'm going to show you how to dig up all this awesome information.

Step #1: Where Are Your Competitors (Both Direct AND Indirect)? Right now, your customers are where your competitors' customers are. So, that's where you need to start looking. You have two types of competitors: direct and indirect. A direct competitor is a person or company selling something very similar to yours. In the supplement business, anyone else selling the same type of supplements is my direct competitor. We are trying to sell basically the same thing to the same people. We're going to do a direct competitor analysis in a moment.

There are also indirect competitors. These are people or companies selling something different than you, but to the same demographic. When I started studying indirect competitors, it was a huge eye-opener for me. I remember one day I found this cool supplement company selling weight-loss products to an older demographic. They were an indirect competitor because we were selling different products (weight-loss supplements for them and nerve pain supplements for me), but we were both going after the same demographic. I put their website into the tool I'm about to show you, and it opened up a whole new world of places to advertise and types of ads to try. Competitive research is awesome because it can open up new opportunities you never knew about before. For me, each new profitable website I find can be worth tens, if not hundreds, of thousands of dollars a month! So you can see why I spend so much time searching for this buried gold.

The first step is to make a list of your direct and indirect competitors and their landing page URLs. If you don't know who your competitors are, then just go to Google and start typing in search phrases you would want people to type in if they were searching for you. If you're in the weight-loss niche, for example, you'd just type in phrases like "how to lose weight" or "losing weight quickly." Look for the paid ads (usually on the right hand side) and start clicking on those ads. This will give you a good idea of who your successful competitors are. Now that you have your competitors' website URLs, let me show you how simple it is to find out exactly WHERE they are already advertising, WHAT ads they're running, and WHERE they are sending their traffic. Using this simple strategy, you'll quickly be able to figure out all five of the variables in each of the competitors' campaigns.

Step #2: What Are They Doing? There are a few products on the market that will do what I'm about to show you. At the time of my writing this book, my favorite is called SimilarWeb.com (SW). Because I want this book to stay evergreen, I will post a video showing you how to use SW here: www.DotComSecretsBook.com/resources/similarweb, and if my team ever finds software we like better, or if SW stops working, we'll give you the most up-to-date information on that page.

So, the first step is to put in your competitor's website URL. For this example, I will enter one of my own websites for you to see.

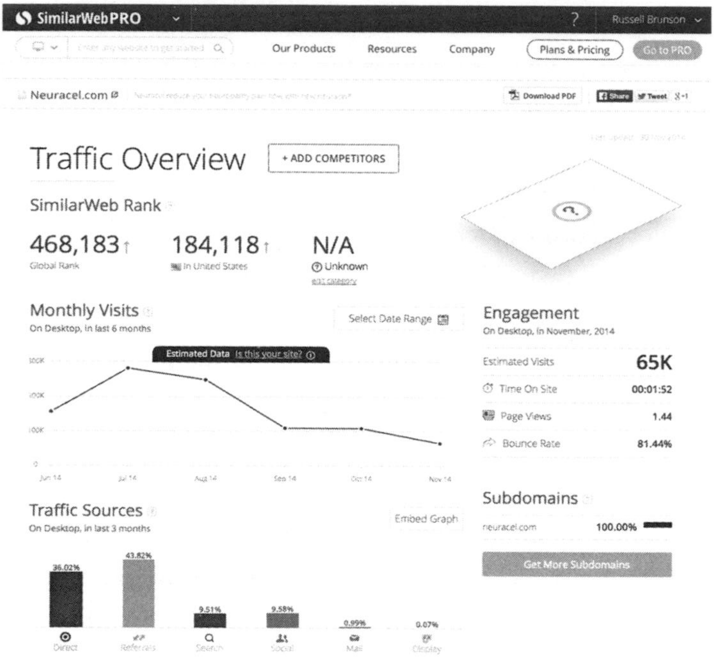

Fig 9.2: It's easy to find your competitors' traffic sources with online tools like Similar Web.

From here, I can quickly see each of the paid traffic sources that the competitor is using.

As I start clicking on some of the other options on the side of the page, I can see the demographics of the traffic that is coming to that website. I can dig deeper into the traffic sources and actually see what sites my ads are running on, when they were first seen, and the duration each ad has been running. (Hint: longer duration=ad that is working.)

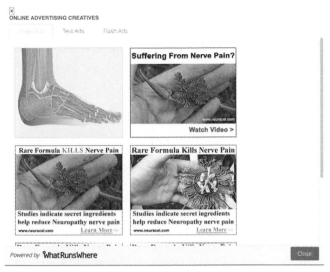

Fig 9.3: Long running ads are usually
high-converting and big money makers.

As I dig deeper, I can start to see the exact banner ads that are working, including the ad copy that is converting.

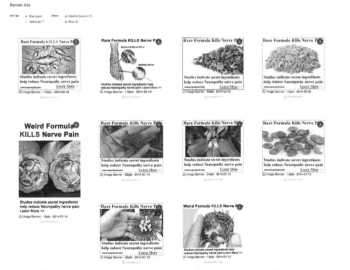

Fig 9.4: Collect the actual ads your competitors
are running and model them for your own ads.

I can also see the landing pages the competitor is pushing the majority of traffic to and a whole bunch more. Do you see how in less than five minutes I can learn EVERYTHING I need to know about a competitor's campaign? I've just shown you how quickly you can grab the five variables we need to be successful:

1. Demographics
2. Offer
3. Landing page
4. Traffic source
5. Ad copy

[handwritten note: NOT AS EASY WITH B2B OR CONSULTING]

The last step is actually to purchase my competitor's product so that I can see the upsells and downsells. What email does this company send to customers? What else happens after the initial purchase? Armed with this information, you now have everything you need to start building out your own successful sales funnels in that niche.

Isn't it amazing? You can literally reverse engineer everything your competitor is doing in less than ten minutes. Just plug in the website and go where they have already gone. Sell to the customers who have already shown interest in this type of product or service. Redirect them to buy your products!

LET'S REVIEW:

1. Make a list of your direct and indirect competitors.
2. Find each landing page URL.
3. Enter a URL into the online research tools.
4. Collect data, dig deep, click on links, buy products, and see what the competitor is doing.
5. Create a swipe file of ideas to model.

To help you out, I've created a checklist you can download and keep handy while you're researching. With this checklist, you'll be sure not to miss any critical components of your research. To download the checklist, go to www.DotComSecretsBook.com/resources/reverse.

Up Next: Now that you've had a chance to look at what your competitors' sales funnels look like, I want to walk you through the seven phases of all successful sales funnels. This will give you a very clear example of each of the phases that your customers should go through as they ascend your Value Ladder.

SIMILAR WEB

Heavy @ legalitebo
SW LOPEZ 2018

SEVEN PHASES OF A FUNNEL

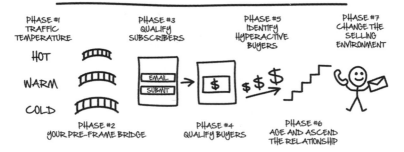

THE 7 PHASES OF A FUNNEL

PHASE #1
TRAFFIC
TEMPERATURE

HOT

WARM

COLD

PHASE #2
YOUR PRE-FRAME BRIDGE

PHASE #3
QUALIFY
SUBSCRIBERS

PHASE #4
QUALIFY BUYERS

PHASE #5
IDENTIFY
HYPERACTIVE
BUYERS

PHASE #6
AGE AND ASCEND
THE RELATIONSHIP

PHASE #7
CHANGE THE
SELLING
ENVIRONMENT

What's the difference between a six-figure, seven-figure, and eight-figure business? When I first started to scale my companies, I thought there must be huge differences between each of these levels, but that's not the case. After going through these levels over the past decade or so, I can tell you the main difference is not what you might think.

- It's not the products you sell.
- It's not the type of business you run—-online or local brick and mortar.
- It's not the traffic.
- It's not the sales copy.
- It's not a high-converting website.
- It's not a product-launch method.

These things are all important. They're all elements of a successful business. But they are not the core difference that sets the levels apart.

The real difference between having a six-, seven-, or even eight-figure business is whether you understand the phases of a funnel and can successfully monetize the different points along the line.

When I'm driving traffic to a website, I need to know the first page the potential customer will hit. I need to know the second page he hits and everything he will experience while he's engaged with my business. I need to carefully engineer the process (or funnel) each customer goes through. And different types of people require different treatment (and different processes).

Lots of people talk about the lifetime value of a customer, but that's not what I'm talking about here. I'm talking about the path that you take your customers down. I'm zeroing in on the variables in each step that can be manipulated for maximum monetization—all while keeping a relationship so that the customer will continue to ascend your Value

Ladder. A person might be with me for a few minutes, a few hours, or dozens of years. The money you make in your business depends on how well you manage the experience of every person who comes in contact with you—no matter how long they stay.

Your goal, of course, is to get the prospect to stick around and become a regular client or repeat buyer. The longer you can keep them around, the more likely they'll buy from you. The way you keep them around is by managing the experience throughout the process. I've broken the customer experience down to seven specific points in the funnel. At each point, you can test, tweak, monetize, and build your business to whatever level you want. Once you know these seven points and how to maximize them, your life will change. It's awesome!

IT'S ALL ABOUT THE PRE-FRAME

Before we talk about the seven phases of a funnel, you need to understand the concept of a pre-frame because each step in a funnel is a pre-frame for the next step. That is why it's essential to optimize these steps—not only for monetization, but also to build relationships and get visitors to continue to buy from you, someone they know and trust. One big mistake many marketers make is focusing 100% on short-term conversions or monetization. They sell so aggressively, focused on the sale at hand, that they lose the respect of their customer. This mistake will cost you the long-term relationship that can be worth ten times as much as the money made through the initial point of contact.

Experts in neuro-linguistic programming (NLP) talk a lot about pre-framing to gain the outcome you desire. A pre-frame is simply the state of mind you place someone in as they enter into the next step in your sales funnel. Changing the frame of mind, the mindset, can profoundly change the answer to a question or the experience you have with someone or something.

People do this all the time without realizing it. For example, if I want to ask my wife a favor, I might pre-frame her by saying, "Wow, you are looking beautiful today. Thanks so much for all the great stuff you're doing with the kids tonight. I really appreciate you spending the evening with them." Then I might follow that up with, "I'm just curious, do you mind if I go hang out with my buddies tonight?" Because I started with the pre-frame, it's more likely that she'll respond the way I want her to. I set up a positive frame of mind before I asked the favor.

My first Internet marketing mentor was a guy named Mark Joyner. I remember him saying that not all clicks are created equal. That struck me as odd because business owners always talk about traffic and how to get more clicks to their websites—not a certain kind of click. Wasn't a click just a click? But Mark made me understand that what really matters most is where those clicks are coming from and what that reader experienced before he got to your site. He even went so far as to say that the frame people enter your website through is probably the most important thing you can know.

He used me as an example: "Consider a person came from a website that said, 'Russell Brunson is a scam artist. He stole my money. He's unethical. He's a liar, and I don't trust him. Click here to see his new product.' What do you think will happen when he clicks through to see the product?" The pre-frame was terrible. That visitor is probably not going to like me, and I will have a hard time getting them to buy anything.

On the other hand, what if the person comes from a site that says, "Russell is an amazing person. I had a chance to meet him; we talked for an hour, and what he taught me changed my business and my life. My company was able to go from nothing to a million dollars of revenue a year. Click here to see his new product"? The chances of converting that potential customer on my site are much, much higher. I can sell more if the visitor enters my website through a good pre-frame. The frame through which he entered my website completely changes what can happen on the actual page. So the trick is to figure out how to control the frame that your traffic is coming through.

In the book *Sway: The Irresistible Pull of Irrational Behavior*, by Ori and Rom Brafman, I read about a fascinating study that took place at MIT, demonstrating the pre-frame principle in action. It went something like this: One day, a class of seventy economics students were told they would have a substitute professor for the day. Since this professor was new, each student was to read a short biography of the teacher. The bios handed out to all the students were identical—except for one phrase. It praised this teacher's graduate work in economics and listed various fabulous accomplishments. Then half the bios described the professor as "a very warm person," while the other half described him as "rather cold." That was the only difference—one phrase.

After the lecture, each student was asked to fill out a survey to see how they liked the teacher. The ones who received the "warm" bio said they loved him. They said he was good natured, considerate of others, and sociable. The students who received the "cold" bio didn't like him at all. They said he was self-centered, formal, irritable, and ruthless. These students all sat through the same lecture, but the pre-frame changed their perception of what they witnessed. This study is such a cool example of the pre-frame principle at work.

How to Pre-Frame Your Presentations for Higher Sales: The first time I witnessed this concept in action was back when I first started speaking at events on Internet marketing. Event coordinators would invite me to speak, and afterward I was allowed to sell my product at the back of the room. Obviously, I wanted to make lots of sales, so I tried to craft my presentation in a way that would deliver such great value that people would want to buy a coaching package from me at the end. I travelled around the country, speaking once or twice a month. Often I would test different pitches to see which method people responded to most.

I remember one event that had a profound effect on me. I was working with a big event promoter named Armand Morin, who had done tons of events all around the world. He was also one of the best stage presenters around at the time. I remember he pulled me aside and said there was one deciding factor that would affect how much money I made at the event. "It's all about how I introduce you," he said.

He asked me to look back at the last ten or fifteen events I worked and remember the events where I did really, really well in sales. Then he said, "Remember back to how the person introduced you before you got on stage. Most promoters do a horrible job. They get up there and say something like, 'Hey, this is Russell. He is great, and he's going to teach you this cool thing. Everyone give him a round of applause.'" When that happens, sales are kind of flat. But this promoter crafted my introduction in a way to pre-sell my credibility as a speaker and get the audience prepared to buy. He had some of the most successful events because of this simple strategy.

I thought his suggestion was really interesting. When I spoke next at his event, I sold more product by far than at any other seminar. Going forward, I paid attention to what happened when promoters introduced me. Sure enough, there would be a drop of energy in the room if the introduction was bland and uninspiring. Everything was different, and it affected my sales. Finally, I decided to be in charge of the pre-frame. I didn't want to run the risk of the promoter screwing it up. So, I made a three-minute introduction video. It featured Tony Robbins recommending me, outlined several success stories, and included the testimony of others who declared I was a great guy with a lot to offer. Before I went on stage, I had the promoter introduce the video. The video played, and then I came up on stage right afterward. The video was the pre-frame, and because I now controlled the frame, I started seeing consistently higher sales almost every time I spoke. Pretty cool, huh? If you speak and sell after each event, give this strategy a try. You'll thank me for it.

Now that you understand pre-framing, you're going to love how powerful the seven phases of a funnel truly are.

HOW PRE-FRAMING WORKS

Many online marketing and conversion trainings start teaching conversion on the landing page. They show you how to split test different designs and how to tweak your offers and your funnels. But I've found there are three critical steps *before* the visitor even gets to the landing page that have a huge effect on your conversions. There are also several steps in the funnel that happen *after* someone leaves your landing page. These also have an enormous impact on your conversions and your bottom line. If you understand all seven points in the funnel, your business will likely explode without any additional traffic or tweaking. So, let's go through the phases one at a time.

Phase #1: Determine Traffic Temperature

The first phase to examine is the mindset of the traffic before it reaches your site—or, your traffic temperature. You may not ever think about it, but there are three levels of traffic that come to your website: hot, warm, and cold. Each group needs special treatment and individualized communication. Each needs to come across a different bridge to arrive at your landing page. Yes, that means you may even need three different landing pages, depending on how you're driving traffic. Trust me, it's worth taking the extra time to set this up correctly.

Here is a quote from Gene Schwartz that helped me to understand hot vs. warm and cold traffic and how you must communicate differently with each type:

If your prospect is aware of your product and has realized it can satisfy his desire, your headline starts with the product. If he is not aware of your product, but only of the desire itself, your headline starts with the desire. If he is not yet aware of what he really seeks, but is concerned with the general problem, your headline starts with the problem and crystallizes it into a specific need.

Unaware → Problem Aware → Solution Aware → Product Aware → Most Aware

COLD ⇒ WARM ⇒ HOT

Fig 10.2: Start your copy wherever your prospect is at the time.

You have to figure out where your prospect is along the product-awareness continuum: product aware, desire aware, or problem aware. Where they are determines the temperature of the traffic. If you have cold traffic, they will probably be aware of the problem they are having, but may not be aware of the solution. For these people, you need to focus your copy on the problem because that's what they're most aware of. Traffic from your blog may be aware of the solution because you presented it in the blog post. So for these people, you want to focus on the solution. Hot traffic from your email list probably knows you and your product, so they would be the most product aware and would respond best to product-based copy.

Hot Traffic is made up of people who already know who you are. They're on your email list, they subscribe to your podcast, they read your blog—you have an established relationship with them. You're going to talk to these people like they're your friends (because they are). You want to use personality-driven communication. Tell them stories, share your opinions, and let them into your private life a little bit. Remember the Seinfeld email examples from the last chapter? They each brought me over one hundred thousand dollars because I had hot traffic, and I knew how to talk to them.

Warm Traffic consists of people who don't know you, but they have a relationship with somebody you know. This is where joint venture (JV) partnerships work well. Affiliates or JV partners have relationships with their lists, and they endorse you or your offer to their subscribers. They lend their credibility to you so their followers feel comfortable checking out your offers.

Direct mail companies have used this pre-framing technique for decades. Different companies have their own house lists, and sometimes one company would mail out a sales letter for someone else's product. Just like joint ventures today, the companies usually split the profit 50/50. To achieve a positive pre-frame, the company that owned the list would add what's called a "lift letter." This was just a personal note saying something like, "Hey, I like this product. I endorse it. This company is great; you won't be sorry if you order from them." Lift letters increased ("lifted") response dramatically because the person reading it had some sort of relationship with the writer or the company giving the recommendation. One good pre-frame can make a page convert like crazy, but when you try to drive cold traffic to it, it bombs.

Cold Traffic is made up of people who have no idea who you are. They don't know what you offer or whether they can trust you. These may be people you find on Facebook or who click on your pay-per-click ads. Maybe they stumble across your blog somehow. Most likely, you're paying for this traffic somehow, so it's important to pre-frame them correctly to get the highest return on your investment.

The first step is to figure out what temperature your traffic is so that you can build the right pre-frame bridge.

Phase #2: Set Up the Pre-Frame Bridge

The second phase is your pre-frame bridge. This might be a pay-per-click ad or it might be an article in an email or a blog post. It might be a YouTube video. It's a bridge that pre-frames people before they get to your landing page. Different types of traffic need different bridges.

A **Hot Traffic Bridge** is typically very short. You already have a relationship with these people, so you don't have to do a lot of credibility building or pre-framing. You can probably just send out a quick email with a link to your landing page, and that's about it. Or maybe you write a blog post or record a podcast encouraging people to go check out your offer. These people will listen and do as you suggest simply because they already know, like, and trust you.

A **Warm Traffic Bridge** is a little longer than a hot traffic bridge, but not much. All that traffic needs is a little note of endorsement from a person they trust; then they'll be in the right frame of mind to go to the landing page. This is where the lift letter or personal email from a JV partner comes in. This bridge could be an email, but it could also be a video, article, or some other communication from the list owner, endorsing you and your product.

A **Cold Traffic Bridge** is the holy grail of online marketing. If you really want to scale your business, you have to learn how to convert cold traffic. Most people I know just can't do this. They can convert like crazy with their own list or a partner's list. But when it comes to converting a cold list, they're stuck. They just can't make it work. If you learn this one skill—converting cold traffic—you'll know the secret behind growing seven-, eight-, or even nine-figure businesses. This bridge is the longest. You need to do a good bit of preliminary work to get the prospect into a desirable frame of mind *before* he hits your landing page. Let me explain.

Let's say you're at the food court in the mall, and you walk up to people waiting in line at Panda Express and say, "Hi there. I'm selling this product that teaches you how to build a list and drive traffic to it.

It's great! Would you be interested in buying it?" What do you think they're going to say? First of all, they don't know you, so the chances of them saying yes are pretty slim. But in addition to that, you're talking in a language they may not even understand. Do these strangers know what a list is? How about traffic? They might think you're talking about highway traffic. This is a huge mistake, and I see businesses make this misstep online all the time. They talk to cold traffic in the wrong language, and nobody buys. To fix this, you need to make your offer more general. Talk in terms that cold traffic will understand.

For example, I have a membership site called ListHacking. It teaches people how to make money by building a list and driving traffic. For our cold traffic, I knew we couldn't talk in terms of "traffic" and "lists" right off the bat. First, we had to explain those concepts so the reader would know what we were talking about. My team developed a different funnel for cold traffic that started out saying, "Who wants a free money-making website?" Once they got the free website, we sent them to a bridge page that said, "Thanks for requesting your website; you'll be receiving it shortly. While we have your attention, do you know how to get people to visit your website?" (Notice I said *people*, not *traffic.)* Then the page goes on to explain that in online sales, potential customers are "traffic." We further explain that in order for them to make money on this new, free website, they must learn how to get traffic to the site. We continue explaining the topic of traffic and lists on the bridge page. Now, when the "cold" visitor does cross over to the membership site offer, they are perfectly pre-framed to understand the offer. That understanding makes them more likely to convert. I bridged the knowledge gap using a pre-frame.

For hot and warm traffic, the ad or email generally serves as the pre-frame. There's no need for extra steps before those people understand your offer. They already know, like, and trust you. But for cold traffic, you often need a whole separate page that they go through (the bridge page) before they hit the offer page. As I just explained, this separate, pre-frame page educates people, enabling them to better appreciate the offer and making them more likely to convert.

Here's another example from my supplement company. One of the products we sell is a supplement to help with neuropathy pain. If I have a list of neuropathy sufferers, it's pretty easy to convert them. But what if someone on my list doesn't have neuropathy as a common characteristic, or doesn't *know* whether they have it? Many people know they have nerve pain, but have never heard the word *neuropathy*. So our cold traffic offer helps people with *nerve pain*, a simpler, more relatable term. My pre-frame page states, "If you have nerve pain, it's probably caused by neuropathy." Then the page goes on to explain a bit about the unfamiliar term. Then, when the visitor gets to the funnel's landing page, all the language suddenly makes sense. They now understand that the nerve pain is due to neuropathy, and our supplement can help. What happens when we do that? Our universe of potential customers expands exponentially! Whatever product you're selling, it's critical that you match your message to your traffic's temperature and knowledge. This awareness will help you determine the kind of bridge required to take them to the landing page.

Blogs are another great way to pre-frame an offer. Often we'll contact someone who's gone through our business program and been successful. We'll sometimes pay them to write a blog post, testifying to the incredible experience. They can then post this praise on their blog. Next, we drive traffic to that blog post so readers see the recommendation and then click over to our product. Because the traffic is coming from the pre-frame of somebody else's site, we dramatically increase our conversions. We are now tapping into the group of people who know and trust the blogger.

We can do the same thing with YouTube testimonials. If someone puts up their own video about one of our products, we'll ask them to add some keywords to the description and add a link back to our product's site. Then we drive traffic to the YouTube video that shares the story. Now the traffic comes to our site with a better chance of converting. Our conversion numbers in these scenarios are crazy high simply because of the positive pre-frame.

Another cool type of bridge page is a survey or a quiz. We can ask certain questions to get the mind's wheels spinning in a particular direction. We plant seeds, and the visitors start wondering about a question we asked. Then they click over to the landing page where we reveal the answer or solution. It's all about influencing what people are thinking about when they see your offer.

Phase #3: Qualify Subscribers

The whole goal here is to take all the traffic—hot, warm, and cold—and find out who is willing to give us an email address in exchange for more information. (This is known as subscribing to a list.) If people aren't willing to give their email addresses at this point, they are highly unlikely to give me money later. Qualifying subscribers is done through an opt-in or squeeze page that offers something of value in return for contact information. This is typically the very frontend of your Value Ladder. For my companies, it's usually a free report or a free video showing the visitor one thing they would really want to know. Let's say I have one thousand visitors who come to my site each day. If I have a 30% conversion rate at this point, then I know I have about three hundred people who will be interested in my information. Now I have a list of warm leads, and I can continue to move them through the rest of my funnel.

Phase #4: Qualify Buyers

Immediately after you qualify your subscribers, you want to find out who among them is a buyer. How many of those three hundred people who were interested in getting free information are willing to pull out their credit cards and make a purchase? Notice I said you must find your potential buyers *immediately* after you qualify subscribers. Don't wait a day or a week. Qualify buyers right away. My early mentor Dan Kennedy taught me this golden principle: *a buyer is a buyer is a buyer.* If someone is willing to buy from you once, they'll continue to buy from you as long as you keep offering value. So as soon as someone fills out their name and email address and clicks the submit button, they should land on a page that offers something to buy. Offer them something of value that will hook them. It's typically a little higher up your Value Ladder, and this is where I'm usually selling my "bait," which is something your dream clients will really love. It should be priced so low that it's an absolute no-brainer for them to buy. You want to qualify every buyer on the list, so don't put up any barriers.

I usually use a "free-plus-shipping" offer or something in the five to seven dollar range. The offer is extremely cheap because I want all the buyers to go for it. Once I've identified who the buyers are, then I can market to them differently. I can pick up the phone and talk to them; I can send them a postcard or add them to a separate email sequence. At this point, I have two lists: subscribers and buyers. Each list is unique and gets treated differently.

Phase #5: Identify Hyperactive Buyers

After you've identified the buyers, you want to identify the *hyperactive* buyers. These are the people who are in some kind of pain right now and will buy more than one thing at a time. I'm often a hyperactive buyer myself. I remember taking my team bowling for a company party a while back. Now, bowling happens to be my third favorite sport (behind wrestling and jiu-jitsu). I'm not a superstar bowler, but I can hold my own. I love playing the game. That particular day, I brought my own ball, gloves, and shoes. I'll admit I kind of wanted to show off in front of my employees. Well, that day one of the other guys had the magic touch. He bowled an awesome couple of games, and he just plain beat me. He was razzing me in front of all my team, and I remember feeling so frustrated. I can laugh at it now, but at the time, I really didn't like it. So I went home and got online and started buying bowling stuff—books, videos, a new ball—anything that would alleviate my humiliating defeat. I was a hyperactive buyer!

You want to identify these people as quickly as possible. Who's in pain right now? And what are they willing to buy *right now* to alleviate that pain? You want to be able to offer them something—ideally several somethings. If you don't, they'll leave your site and go find another site to buy from. People love to buy. And when they're in pain and want relief, they will spend money in that quest. I forgot about bowling a few days later, and life continued on. I was no longer a hyperactive buyer of bowling merchandise. The window closed. So think about what you can upsell or downsell after your initial offer. If you've bought any of my products, you know I always have a chain of upsells and downsells. That's because I want to identify my hyperactive buyers. Once I know who they are, I'm going to treat them differently, too.

Phase #6: Age and Ascend the Relationship

At this point, the initial sales experience is pretty much over. Points one through five all happen in five or ten minutes, and the next two points explain what keeps those people you've identified coming back to buy from you again and again. These next steps are what keeps them referring you to friends. During this step, you want to age and ascend the relationship. Remember your Value Ladder? This is where that ladder of products and services really becomes important. If you've followed the five phases of the funnel up to here, you've already moved people through the first level or two (or three) on your Value Ladder. Now, you're going to continue to provide value and help people with whatever you offer.

Allow some time to pass. How much time is up to you; whatever feels logical for your product is best. Let them dig into whatever products they've already purchased, and give them enough time to see the value you give. You're going to ascend them up the ladder over a longer period of time, eventually moving them to the very top level.

This is the point where we start changing the types of funnels we use. If we started with a Free-Plus-Shipping Funnel, we may move the buyer into an Invisible Funnel or maybe bump them up to a Three-Step, High-Ticket Backend Program. (Don't worry; you're going to learn how to build these different funnels in the second half of this book.)

Phase #7: Change the Selling Environment

Typically, it's difficult to sell super-expensive products or services online. Not many people are going to read a sales letter and click the buy button for a fifteen thousand dollar product. Some might, but usually you have to change the selling environment if you want to sell high-ticket products. The most common ways to change the environment are to sell the pricier items over the phone, through direct mail, or at a live event or seminar. If I send an email out to you and ask you to click an eight thousand dollar buy button, you're probably not going to do it. But if I can get you to click a button and schedule an appointment to chat on the phone, suddenly I have a completely different sales environment. People on the phone are more likely to listen closely to an offer. The sales person has the benefit of live feedback. He or she can overcome objections and help people make up their minds on the fly. When we change the selling environment, we can communicate at a different level, and it becomes easier to move people up to the higher levels of the Value Ladder.

Let's Review: If I were to consult with a retail store on how to increase sales, I would look at everything that happens during a customer's experience with the store, including the moment a customer saw the ad, walked in the front door, and received a greeting from the employees. I would analyze what the customer saw that made them choose certain items, what products were "point of sale," and how the cashier upsold them during checkout. I would then analyze the follow-up sequences already in place to bring that customer back.

Increasing online sales happens the same way. You need to break out and examine each of the phases your customer passes through in your sales funnels. After you are aware of the distinct steps and break each out into a separate experience, you can then tweak each aspect to get more conversions. In this way, you can help people ascend to the next level of your Value Ladder. If you're stuck in your business, it's probably because there's a glitch in one of these seven steps. What's the temperature of the traffic you're driving? What's the pre-frame bridge you're taking potential buyers through? On the landing page, are you qualifying subscribers? Are you qualifying your buyers on the sales page, and your hyperactives on the upsell pages? Are you aging and ascending the relationship to match the buyer with the offer they really need the most? And are you changing the selling environment for your high-ticket offers? Most importantly, how are you treating each of your different groups so that each receives a specially tailored experience?

Up Next: Now that you understand the strategy behind the seven phases of a sales funnel, I want to show you what types of web pages we use for four of those phases. Did you like to play with Lego blocks when you were a kid? I did. It was so cool to take the same, simple pieces and create something totally unique, over and over again. In the upcoming chapters, you're going to learn how to build sales funnels Lego-style. In fact, I'm going to give you a list of building blocks that you can simply mix and match to build your offer to create an instant sales funnel. Then I'm going to give you some short cuts—the exact funnels and scripts I use most often in my businesses. You can copy and paste your own offers and ideas into these proven templates and have your business up and running in no time.

THE TWENTY-THREE BUILDING BLOCKS OF A FUNNEL

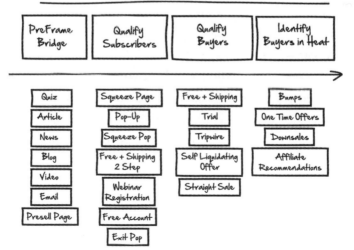

THE 23 BUILDING BLOCKS OF A FUNNEL

PreFrame Bridge	Qualify Subscribers	Qualify Buyers	Identify Buyers in Heat
Quiz	Squeeze Page	Free + Shipping	Bumps
Article	Pop-Up	Trial	One Time Offers
News	Squeeze Pop	Tripwire	Downsales
Blog	Free + Shipping 2 Step	Self Liquidating Offer	Affiliate Recommendations
Video	Webinar Registration	Straight Sale	
Email	Free Account		
Presell Page	Exit Pop		

As I said, I think of sales and building funnels kind of like playing with Legos. I imagine there's this big box of brightly colored building blocks, and I can put them together any way I want to get the desired results. If I want to get someone to opt-in to my list, I might use a yellow block and connect it to a blue block. If I want to make a high-ticket sale, I might add on green, red, and purple blocks. If I'm not getting the results I want, but I know I have all the right pieces, I might rearrange the blocks and see what happens.

This is the exact same process I teach my twenty-five-thousand-dollar clients. I go through each phase of the funnel and map out which building blocks will yield the best results. Then we test the funnels to see how well they convert. Sometimes we hit a winner right away, but often we need to move the blocks around a bit; for example, we might change some copy or add a video. Then we test the combination again. This is how direct response marketers have created magic for over a hundred years: Try it. Test it. Tweak it. And start all over again.

There are two types of Lego sets. You can buy all the blocks and create your own work of art using your imagination. Or you can buy special kits that give you the pieces you need to build specific things, like the Death Star or the Bat Cave. These kits even give you instructions on which piece to attach where and in what order. If you're the kind of person who loves the Lego kits, you're going to love our funnel-building software called ClickFunnels. All the pieces you need are inside the software, easily enabling you to create all sorts of funnels to sell everything from a simple opt-in to a high-end consulting package. And all you have to do is pick which cool thing you want to build and click a button. All the pieces are automatically arranged in the right order for you. If you'd like to try it out, you can get a free two-week trial at www.ClickFunnels.com.

This chapter is going to show you twenty-three of the most effective building blocks for your sales funnels. You will find that certain blocks work better at certain points on your Value Ladder, but remember, they are just blocks. You can move them around as you please. Markets respond according to a huge variety of factors. What works in my world might need a little tweaking in yours.

In the upcoming chapters, I'm going to show you some of my favorite ways to connect the blocks to create working sales funnels. I highly recommend you start with my version, simply because I've tested these in the real world over and over. I know what works in general. Then if you want to try moving things around, go for it! You may discover an approach I never thought of before.

The twenty-three blocks I use most often are used at specific times during four specific phases in the funnel: the pre-frame bridge, qualifying subscribers, qualifying buyers, and identifying hyperactive buyers. Remember, these four points all happen at the point of sale. Any time you sell anything through a funnel (which should be most of the time), you're going to move your buyer through these four points. Most often, you'll be creating new funnels during the *age and ascend* and *change selling environment* phases. When you do that, simply go back to these building blocks and create a new funnel.

Okay, let's get started.

PRE-FRAME BRIDGE
The following are the most common building blocks I use for pre-frames. Remember, the goal with a pre-frame is to warm up the prospects so they are in the correct frame of mind to be most receptive to your offer.

> **Quizzes:** A quiz is my new favorite pre-frame tool. If you're on Facebook, it's difficult to escape all the "What famous actor are you?" or "What jungle animal are you?" quizzes. They seem to get more and more ridiculous all the time. (This morning, I saw one that asked, "What type of storm are you?" Really.)

The questions you ask don't matter much; you just want to get people engaged in the process.

To get a great pre-frame, you want to get people thinking along the same lines as the next step in the funnel. Agitate the problem your business solves for them. Use the quiz questions to help them remember how much they hate weeds in their lawn or being rejected by women. One technique I love to use is to frame the first question like this:

Fig 11.1: A simple pre-frame quiz before someone joins your email list.

If you require people to opt-in (give you an email address) to get their quiz results, you've killed two birds with one stone. The prospect has moved through both the pre-frame and the qualify subscribers phases in the funnel. Then you try to qualify him as a buyer by making an offer immediately after he opts-in.

Now, you may be wondering how many questions to include and how to get people to stay with the quiz all the way to the end. I like to use three or four questions, and I number each one so they know how much farther they have to go (Step

1 of 4, Step 2 of 4 . . .). I do know some companies that use up to twenty questions or more in their quizzes with great success. Just like everything else, this is something you might want to test out to determine what is right for your unique market.

Another great reason to use quizzes is that you can segment your audience according to their answers. You might ask, "Do you have a dog or a cat?" Then you segment your list according to the responses. With sophisticated quiz programs, you can even have the subsequent questions match the two segments. So, your next question to the "dog" segment of responders might be, "How old is your dog?" Then offer answer choices like zero to one, under five years, under ten years, over ten years, etc. How does this help you sell more pet food? Well, puppies need different nutrition than older dogs. If you know how old their dog is, you can sell them exactly the right type of food. Also, if you know the quiz taker has a dog, not a cat, the ad on the next page should picture a dog. The quiz helps you segment your buyers, as well as pre-frame your offer.

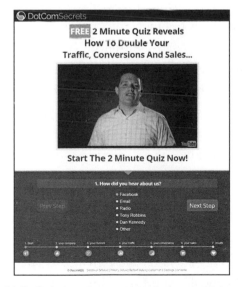

FIG 11.2: Quizzes are great tools for engaging your audience and getting their brains primed for your sales page.

Articles: I love to use articles as a pre-frame for cold traffic coming from a banner ad. These can be articles on your website, but I find they're more effective if they appear on someone else's site. It's like a third-party endorsement. Here's how it works.

Someone clicks your banner ad and lands on a website with a pre-frame article. It might be a case study of how you helped an individual solve a problem. It might be an article about how your product works. Or it might not have anything to do with you specifically, but it sets up the problem and what is required to solve that problem.

Then you add a call to action somewhere on the page. A call to action is simply where you ask the reader to do something: click here to learn more, subscribe today, get your free sample here. In an article, the call to action can be a simple link inside the text, a big button at the bottom of the article, a photo with a link, or a combination of these.

Now, don't be unethical here. For a while, many Internet marketers used this technique successfully with fake news sites and fake blogs that they controlled. The FTC cracked down on that practice, and you really don't want them on your case. Use legitimate articles on legitimate websites. Encourage one of your best students to write an article about you, then use that as the landing page people will see once they click on a banner ad.

News: Anything that's news *or is perceived as news* commands more attention than other reading matter. Our brains are programmed to pay special attention to anything that might be a threat. This is why everything on the evening news is a "Special Alert" or "Disaster Update." Each headline is phrased to get our attention and convince us a developing event is sure to destroy the world as we know it. If your pre-frame is attached somehow to a current news story, you'll automatically receive a bump in attention for as long as that story continues to dominate the news. For example, if you manage to tie your message to an upcoming election or natural disaster, people will see the connection and pay more attention to you as a result. The downside to this strategy is that the recognition can be short lived. However, the upside can be a massive upsurge in traffic while the story is hot.

You can also design the web page to look like a news page. It might have a special bar with a headline on the bottom or a sidebar with a relevant side story. Marketers have found that

Fig 11.3: Articles on news sites lend a feeling of authority to your products and services.

just formatting their content to look like news can increase their credibility and pre-frame their offers nicely. Again, don't go crazy with this strategy, or you'll have the FTC on your case. Besides, it's just bad for business. Be ethical. Tell the truth.

Blogs: A blog post can be used to pre-frame most any topic. For example, maybe you work in a crowded industry with many competitors who all provide basically the same solution. You could write a blog post explaining how every other company is the same, while yours is different and better. You might write the article yourself and post it on your blog. But you'll probably get better results if you guest post it on someone else's blog, preferably a high-traffic blog with lots of visitors in your target market. Better yet, have the blog author post the article in their name so that you are not seemingly tied to it at all. I did this once with a successful student in the "make-money-online" market. I asked him to write an article detailing his experience using my products. He added a link to our offer, and we drove Facebook traffic to his blog post. The campaign worked great. It was engineered as a pre-frame, but the content was 100% true and ethical.

Videos: YouTube videos make great pre-frame material, especially for testimonials. The video should agitate the problem for the viewer or educate them on some process or idea. The goal is to make them desire the solution you offer. Again, have the video appear on someone else's channel and drive traffic there. Then include calls to action that move people to your offer. The calls to action might be links in the description or comments, some pre-roll or post-roll footage, or even annotations in the video.

Email: Pre-framing with email works well when you buy a solo ad or use JV partners to endorse you to their lists. No matter whose list you're mailing to, you're essentially borrowing their credibility to pre-frame you as a great person or to pre-frame your offer as a great solution. Once the pre-frame is accomplished, the call to action is a link in the email that readers can click on to get to your offer. With direct mail, this is done with a lift letter where the owner of the list writes an introduction telling his people how great you are or how well your product works. JV partners or affiliates do the same thing with email by writing an introduction for you or your offer.

Fig 11.4: Presell pages educate the visitor
before they land on your sales page.

Presell Pages: Sometimes you have to educate people before you sell to them. A presell page tells a story. It's a longer article used to give background information or education that prospects might need. Once they have this information, they are in the right frame of mind to understand and buy the offer. For example, maybe you sell email marketing software, but some of your prospects don't know what email marketing is or why their businesses need it. You might send them to a presell page on your website that explains exactly how email marketing helps grow businesses. Then you add a call to action, which will take them to your product offer. This strategy works great for affiliates who want to warm up the prospect before sending them straight over to someone else's sales page.

QUALIFYING SUBSCRIBERS

The next phase is to qualify your subscribers. Remember the goal here is simply to get people to opt-in to your list, subscribe to your newsletter, or request a free offer you've put in front of them. You're separating out the casual visitors from the people who are willing to trade their email addresses in return for more information.

Pop-Ups: Remember years ago when those annoying little boxes popped up on your screen almost every time you visited a website? "Congratulations! You just won . . . blah, blah, blah." They may have been annoying, but they worked like crazy to get people to opt in to a list. Thanks to pop-up blockers and ad blockers, this method became almost obsolete for years, and marketers all but abandoned them. But recently new types of pop-ups have been created that aren't as easily blocked, and we're finding that these pop-ups are becoming a good tool for building a list in many situations. The bigger problem is that some advertisers (like Google and Facebook) won't approve ads that go to pages with pop-ups. So this method doesn't work all the time, but pop-ups can be powerful tools under the right circumstances.

Fig 11.5: Pop-ups can still be effective if used carefully.

Squeeze Page: The squeeze page is the simplest way to qualify subscribers. It was developed as a way to increase subscribers without using pop-ups. It's a simple opt-in page that requires people to give you their email addresses to get access to something on the next page (i.e., a free report or a free video). The only choices on the page are to subscribe or leave. The magic of a squeeze page is the complete lack of distractions. There are no ads to look at and no navigation menu tabs to click. People are forced to focus on your most important message—

the one message you want to give them. And they have to make a decision: either give you their email address or leave the page.

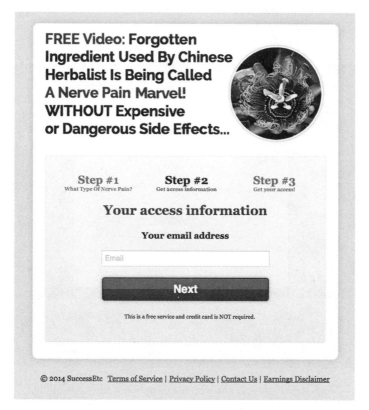

FREE Video: **Forgotten Ingredient Used By Chinese Herbalist Is Being Called A Nerve Pain Marvel! WITHOUT Expensive or Dangerous Side Effects...**

Step #1
What Type Of Nerve Pain?

Step #2
Get access information

Step #3
Get your access!

Your access information

Your email address

Email

Next

This is a free service and credit card is NOT required.

© 2014 SuccessEtc   Terms of Service | Privacy Policy | Contact Us | Earnings Disclaimer

Fig 11.6: A squeeze page has only one goal—to get the visitor to subscribe or request information.

Click Pop: The click pop is a way to get people to join your list via a button on your blog or other web pages. When they click on that button, up pops a squeeze-page-style pop-up. If a visitor gives you their email address, they are taken to the next page. Click pop buttons are great because you can place them in a ton of places, places where you traditionally wouldn't be able to get opt-ins, like articles and blog posts.

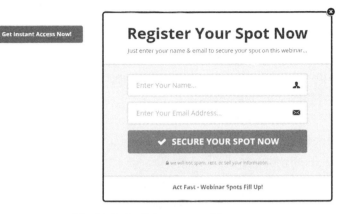

Fig 11.7: A click-pop combines a
clickable button with a pop-up web form.

Free-Plus-Shipping, Two-Step Form: This type of web form takes advantage of buyer psychology and combines the "qualify subscribers" and "qualify buyers" steps into one

Fig 11.8: A two-step web form allows you to collect a name and email address on step one and credit card information on step two.

sequence. Step one qualifies subscribers by asking for contact information (including email addresses). Step two qualifies buyers by asking for credit card information, usually to cover shipping costs. That is how my company structures most of our free-plus-shipping offers.

Anyone who fills out step one of this form is automatically added to an email list and is qualified as a subscriber—even if he doesn't fill out step two.

Webinar Registration: We often use free webinars as a way to generate leads. When people register for the webinar, they naturally need to give you their email addresses because you need to send them details about the webinar. If it's an automated webinar, they pick which day they want to watch, fill in their email, and Boom! A new subscriber is on your list. And because they signed up for a webinar, they'll be looking for your email.

Fig 11.9: Webinar registrations are a natural way to collect email addresses because people expect you to send them more information about the webinar via email.

Free Account: Signing people up for a free account works especially well with software and membership programs. Create a membership site, or a "lite" version of your software, and give it to people for free. When visitors create an account to get access to the membership or the software, they are added to your subscriber list. Often times, these types of pages are very similar to squeeze pages, but because they are actually "creating an account," you can get a lot more information and still keep your conversions high.

(COS FREE VERSION W/ CHECKLIST only?)

Fig 11.10: Free accounts allow you to collect more personal information about a subscriber like physical address and phone number.

Exit Pop: An exit pop is, not surprisingly, a last-chance pop-up after people click away from your site. It asks if they're sure they really want to leave without subscribing. You may even make a special offer to people if they decide to subscribe before they close the exit pop. Once people leave your site, there's a good chance they'll never come back. So, you can afford to annoy them a little bit with an exit pop. It may be your last chance to keep them engaged with you.

Fig 11.11: You can use exit pops as a final appeal to the visitor to give you their email address.

QUALIFYING BUYERS

When we qualify buyers, remember that the goal is to get people to pull out their credit cards and actually pay for something. The first purchase is the hardest to get, so it's best to offer something of value for a very low price. Then, you can guide buyers up the Value Ladder as soon as you can. Here are my favorite ways to qualify buyers:

Free-Plus-Shipping: This is my favorite way to qualify buyers (as you'll see in Secret #13). If you create a great product and give it away for free, it is the perfect bait and gets one of your products into the hands of a new customer. There is no better way than a free-plus-shipping offer to provide value up front and get the buyer interested in ascending. I feel like this tactic is the best way to find out which of your subscribers are also buyers.

Trial: A very low-cost trial offer is a great way to get people to raise their hands and tell you that they're buyers. The easiest and most popular trial is offered for one dollar. Then, you bill them a few days later for the full amount—if they want to keep the product. To receive the trial, a visitor must pull their credit card out of their wallet and prove they are a buyer. This works best for items you don't have to ship, like digital downloads, software, or membership sites.

Tripwire: Tripwires are smaller offers used to get buyers in the door. They are often a "splinter" of your core product. For example, you might pull out one module or one of the training sessions and offer it for a huge discount. Ryan Deiss and Perry Belcher made this technique popular. They usually use a very low-cost offer of around seven dollars per item. These can be physical products or digital downloads, depending on your market.

Self-Liquidating Offers (SLO): These types of offers are usually a little more expensive—between thirty-seven and ninety-seven dollars. Often times, with free-plus-shipping, trials, and tripwire offers, you may actually lose money initially, although through your upsells you can often break even. With a self-liquidating offer, on the other hand, the goal is to have the frontend product liquidate your ad costs so that your upsells can become pure profit.

Straight Sale: This is just a regular sale of a high-ticket item, from ninety-seven to five thousand dollars or higher. It usually takes a little more selling to convert these offers, so we typically only introduce this option to people who are in our warm market or who have gone through our initial funnels. It usually takes a stronger bond with the Attractive Character before people will make these larger investments.

Many people ask me what type of offer they should use to qualify their buyers. Most of the time, I like to use the free-plus-shipping offer to qualify my buyers, but it doesn't always work. We tried this with our neuropathy supplement, and the numbers never quite worked out. So we changed it to a straight sale, and it worked great. Sometimes you try something that doesn't work, so you change the offer. Simply shift to one of the other building blocks, and you could have a winner. You have to test each product. Different markets respond differently, so don't give up on finding interested buyers too soon.

IDENTIFY HYPERACTIVE BUYERS

To figure out which customers are hyperactive buyers at the point of sale, I need to offer an upsell immediately after I qualify them with a low-cost or free offer. Here are my favorite ways to do that:

> **Bumps:** These are the little offers we add on to our order forms, and they have completely transformed our business. This concept is very similar to the experience you have in a grocery store checkout line. You see the candy bars, gum, and other little things that are all too easy to throw in with your order. My team does a similar thing with our order-form bumps. With two lines of text and a checkbox, we are often able to get up to 40% of our buyers to upgrade and pay an extra thirty-seven dollars or more at the point of sale.

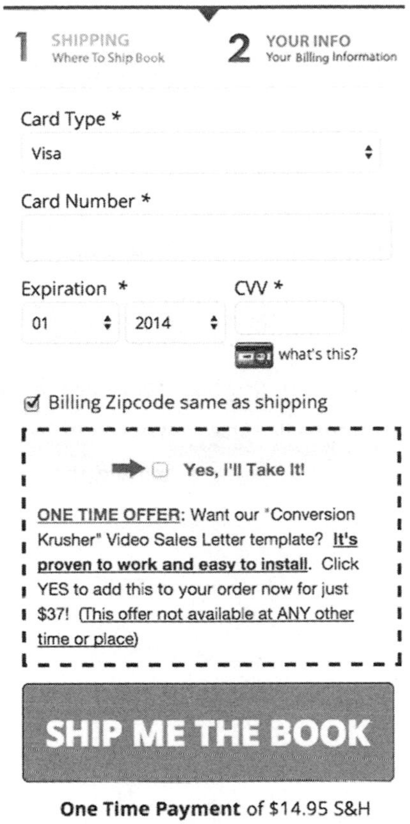

1 SHIPPING
Where To Ship Book

2 YOUR INFO
Your Billing Information

Card Type *

Visa ▲▼

Card Number *

Expiration *   CVV *

01 ▲▼   2014 ▲▼

▭▭ what's this?

☑ Billing Zipcode same as shipping

➡ ☐ Yes, I'll Take It!

ONE TIME OFFER: Want our "Conversion Krusher" Video Sales Letter template? **It's proven to work and easy to install.** Click YES to add this to your order now for just $37! (This offer not available at ANY other time or place)

SHIP ME THE BOOK

One Time Payment of $14.95 S&H

Fig 11.12: Bumps are a subtle way to increase sales (sometimes dramatically). Just make a simple discount offer with a checkbox on the order form.

One-Time Offers (OTOs): After someone has purchased any of your frontend offers, you can make them a special, one-time offer. The best OTOs are products that will complement the initial purchase. Often we'll make two to three separate offers to people after they buy, as long as the sequence of offers adds more value to the initial offer.

Fig 11.13: One Time Offers (OTOs) appear after someone has purchased your first offer. These are special deals they can only get if they act right away.

Downsales: If the buyer says no to the OTO, you can downsell them with either a different product or a payment plan option on the original offer. Don't give up just because they said no to paying the full amount all at once. Often we find that up to 20% of people who say no to the special offer will say yes to a payment-plan version on a downsell.

Affiliate Recommendations: These recommendations typically happen after buyers finish going through my upsale/

downsale sequenece and have landed on the "thank you" page in my funnel. On this page, I will usually thank buyers for ordering and then link to other offers that would likely serve them.

Let's Review: Do you see how these blocks work to build a system that benefits your company? Simply go through each phase in the funnel and choose which block you want to try. You'll soon discover the ones that work best in your market, and you'll rely on them over and over. But don't forget to test out some of the alternatives now and then. You never know when a straight sale will beat out a trial for a particular offer—unless you test it. I encourage you to split test different blocks for all your offers. I know split testing can be intimidating for some, and the software can be expensive. But I think it's so important to the long-term growth of your business that we included simple split testing options inside ClickFunnels to make it super easy.

Up Next: New ideas for building blocks are being developed all the time, but these listed above are the most common and most effective, I've found. Now that you know what the blocks are, we can start building actual funnels.

In the next chapter, I'm going to discuss which types of funnels we use on the frontend of our Value Ladders, the ones we use in the middle, and those we use for the backend. Understanding this will help you to better understand how to use each of the funnels I will be giving you later.

FRONTEND VS. BACKEND FUNNELS

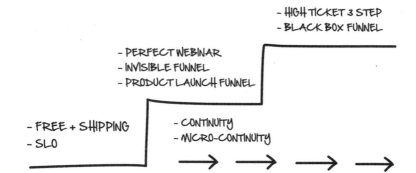

FRONTEND VS BACKEND FUNNELS

- HIGH TICKET 3 STEP
- BLACK BOX FUNNEL

- PERFECT WEBINAR
- INVISIBLE FUNNEL
- PRODUCT LAUNCH FUNNEL

- FREE + SHIPPING
- SLO

- CONTINUITY
- MICRO-CONTINUITY

N ow that you know the building blocks, all you have to do to build your own funnels is put them together. You can combine them any way you like, but I have seven tested and proven funnels that I use all the time with my mastermind clients and with my own companies. We use them over and over and over again, and they work. In section 4, you're going to learn how each of these funnels functions. But before we go there, you need to see how we use different funnels for different steps on the Value Ladder. Funnels have a psychology behind them, and you need to use a different psychological approach for a low-priced, introductory product vs. a high-ticket package.

Product Awareness Continuum: The basic psychology goes back to the product awareness continuum we discussed when we were talking about traffic temperature in Secret #9.

Fig 12.2: How you speak to your prospects depends on where they are on the product awareness continuum.

Cold traffic is probably only aware of the problem they are facing. They don't know you or your products, so they need to start at the front of the Value Ladder with a low-level funnel, like a Free-Plus-Shipping or Self-Liquidating-Offer Funnel. These funnels are proven to work on cold traffic, people who don't know you or the solution you're providing.

These potential customers will start to warm up to you after they start going through your communication funnel—building a bond with the Attractive Character. As they do, you can start introducing bigger-ticket products through the funnels we use in the middle of the Value

Ladder. I like to sell these mid-priced offers using a Perfect Webinar Funnel, Invisible Funnel, or Product-Launch Funnel. Each of these takes the time to go into more detail about the solution you're providing with your product, so the sales funnel is a little different.

Hot traffic already knows you, likes you, and trusts you. They know your products, so it's time to direct them to the backend as you focus on the highest level of service you can offer. Because these offers have a greater price, you probably aren't going to be able to close many sales using online methods alone. You need to change the selling environment and get the prospect on the phone or to a live event. My favorite funnel for moving people from the computer to the phone is the High-Ticket, Three-Step Funnel.

In the upcoming chapters, I'm also including my favorite sales scripts to help you write the sales letters and videos you'll need to include in your funnels. You'll want to tweak them by adding in the details for your company and your market. Think of these scripts like a framework—all the elements you need are there, and you simply add in the details.

Before we go through these funnels and scripts, there are a few things to keep in mind:

1. These funnels start on the landing page. They do not cover the traffic temperature or the pre-frame bridge. They are the sales mechanisms designed to move a person from being a completely anonymous visitor to becoming a paying customer. Traffic and pre-frame are important elements, too, so be sure to consider them carefully when deciding which funnel to use.

2. When you're ready to "age and ascend" customers on your Value Ladder, all you have to do is create a new funnel. The people you age and ascend will now be considered warm traffic, so you can treat them like old friends and approach your funnels from that perspective.

3. Some of these funnels and scripts are short and sweet. Some are very long and involved. Generally, the higher up on the Value Ladder you are, the more selling you have to do and the longer your script will be. Although, if you have hot traffic, you can sometimes get away with a less involved script.

THE BIG PICTURE

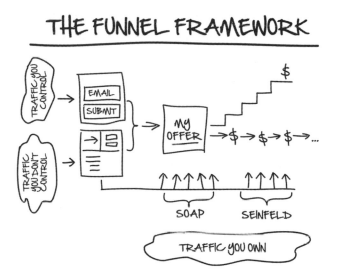

Fig 12.3: The core funnel moves people from the traffic stage all the way up the Value Ladder.

Before we move on to the individual funnels, let's zoom out and look at the big picture, how everything we've talked about so far ties together. Figure 12.3 shows the overall framework of each of our companies.

Traffic that we control, we drive to a squeeze page. Traffic that we don't control, we drive to a blog where the top third of the page collects email addresses. As soon as someone joins, through either of those sources, they become traffic that we own, and we start sending them the Soap Opera Sequence so that they can build a relationship with the

Attractive Character. When that sequence is done, we start sending daily Seinfeld emails to help them ascend through the other offerings on our Value Ladder.

Now, immediately after a person joins my list, through either the squeeze page or the blog, they are taken to my first frontend offer. This is the offer I use to qualify my buyers. Those who purchase that product will immediately see a few point-of-sale upsells.

After that initial transaction is over, my email sequences will start to encourage people to purchase other products as they ascend my Value Ladder and join my continuity programs. I will use different types of funnels to sell people different products in the Value Ladder.

Figure 12.3 shows you the overview of everything we've discussed so far at a higher level. This is how I view companies when I first start working with them. After I see what a business looks like from this high-level view, I can easily see what is broken and then dive into the specifics to get the results the owners want and need.

I encourage you to take what you've learned so far, along with what you are currently doing in your company, and use this image to find your holes. Determine what you need to change or create in order to build your solid foundation.

THE BEST BAIT

THE 100 VISITOR TEST

I have one last thing to share with you before I give you access to my seven proven funnels. I think if you understand this one crucial concept, it will change how you build your sales funnels. When I discovered what I am about to share, it literally changed my company overnight. I went from making about thirty thousand dollars a year online to making over seven figures in less than eighteen months.

THE ONE-HUNDRED-VISITOR TEST

Back when I was twelve years old and a newly addicted junk mail collector, I remember calling 1-800 numbers every day and ordering free information. It didn't matter what the information was about—it was free and I wanted it. Free samples and free trials are everywhere, online and off. Why? Because they work like crazy to get people's attention. Humans just can't resist the word *FREE*.

If you haven't read the book *Predictably Irrational* by Dan Ariely, I highly recommend you pick up a copy and read it. In this book, the author talks about an experiment studying the effects of the word *free* on buying behavior.

You can read about the entire experiment in his book, but here's the relevant part for this chapter: Researchers offered a group of students a Lindt Truffle for twenty-six cents and a Hershey's Kiss for one cent and then observed buying behavior. They found that about 50% of participants went for the Kiss, while 50% chose the Lindt Truffle. When researchers dropped the price of both chocolates by one cent, suddenly 90% of the students took the free Kiss, even though the relative price between the two was still the same. Researchers also ran tests in which they lowered the price from two cents to one cent to see if it increased demand for the Kiss, but it didn't. They ran other tests where they lowered the price from free to negative one cent, but they still didn't see any changes in buying behavior. They ran this same experiment over and over on college students, children, older adults, and more, yet the results stayed the same. There was power in *free*!

I thought that was a pretty cool concept, and it got me excited to implement this concept in my company. I asked myself, *How can I offer something in my business for free?* If everyone in my industry or my town is offering discounted products, but I can offer mine for free, suddenly the majority of people are going to choose me. So, how can I structure my offer to give something away for free?

I started trying things out and testing the results to see which offers I could give away to get the biggest response.

Eventually, I came up with my own experiment to test the effects of offering something for free. I call it my One-Hundred-Visitor Test. I ran it many times in different environments with different target audiences and products, and the results were pretty consistent in almost every test we ran. While we ran this test with hundreds of thousands of website visitors, I broke it down and simplified the findings to show what our core numbers looked like for every hundred visitors we sent through this test funnel.

Here's how it worked: I sent one hundred people to a website where they could purchase a product. The product was offered for $197. We paid a talented copywriter and tested different pitches until we got a high-converting page. After all the testing and tweaking, we wound up getting about 1% of cold traffic to convert and buy the product. So, for every one hundred visitors, we made $197, and we got one new customer on our list. Most marketers would consider that result about average.

Then we started shifting things around and experimented with offering something for free. We wanted to see how this new offer would change the metrics and our income. So, we splintered off one of the best parts of our product and put it into a form we could ship to our customers for free if they'd help cover the shipping costs. We offered to put this information on a CD, a DVD, or a book. After people signed up for the free-plus-shipping offer, then we'd immediately upsell them on the same $197 product we were trying to sell before. I figured I would lose money because I was making people pull out their credit cards and buy the free-plus-shipping offer before they even saw the $197 offer. I mean, if only one-tenth of potential customers ever even saw the $197 offer, logically I should make less money, right?

Here's what happened: We sent people to the website, and on average, a whopping 8% of people purchased the free-plus-shipping offer. (Remember, that's up from 1% on the original page. And the free-plus-shipping page needed almost NO copy to sell, whereas on the original $197 page, we had to include really convincing text to persuade people to buy.)

Now, this is where the magic happens. Because the customer had ALREADY pulled a credit card out of their wallet and made a commitment towards the concept we were selling, about 25% of free-plus-shipping customers bought the upsell offer. That means we made $394 per one hundred visitors, and we got eight new buyers on our list. I almost doubled my money and got seven times more customers by adding in a *free*-plus-shipping offer! Pretty cool, huh?

I don't know what it is about buyer psychology, but once you get someone to say the first yes, it's so much easier to get the second yes. It's a slippery slope. You get them started by saying yes to a small thing, then they are much more likely to say yes to a larger thing later.

People ask me if they can just sell (or just give away) a digital product instead of the free-plus-shipping offer. The answer is yes, you can, but you are missing out on some very powerful things. I like to make the free offer physical because it gives me the ability to use the word *free*, while also requiring the interested customer to pull out their credit card to pay for shipping and qualify as a buyer. If I decide to sell this as a digital product for a small price, then I lose the power of free. And if I just give it away free digitally, then I lose the power of qualifying the buyer when they pay the shipping costs. I also lose the ability to do a one-click upsell on the next page. Does that make sense?

Over the years, this concept has continued to evolve, as you'll see in the coming chapters showing you the funnels. My team started adding multiple upsells after the initial free-plus-shipping offer, and we saw a huge increase in revenues. We also created sales scripts that work almost universally across most of the markets we've tested them in. You'll get to learn more about those funnels and scripts and the evolution of our process in the next section of this book. However, the *biggest* advancement we stumbled upon was the order form bump. Let me explain how it works.

THE FREE-PLUS-SHIPPING ORDER FORM BUMP

After many initial tests, we started testing our free-plus-shipping concept against our thirty-seven dollar products. What we found is so simple, yet it has been one of our biggest secrets to increasing our frontend revenue with almost no effort.

We took our thirty-seven dollar products and tested them against a free CD—a simple audio recording teaching one of the most exciting concepts from the product. We started driving traffic to both landing pages, and we found that, on average, we could get about three times as many customers to pay shipping for the free CD.

So, we had three times as many customers following the "free" route and that meant three times as many people were now seeing our upsell path. But we were missing out on getting our thirty-seven dollar product into the hands of our customers and losing the extra up-front revenue from this frontend product. In other words, we were getting more frontend customers, but our average cart value (how much money you average from each person who goes through your funnel) was lower, making our revenue come out about the same.

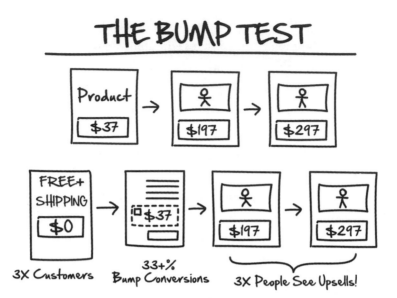

Fig 13.1a: Order form bumps take about five minutes to implement and can dramatically improve your bottom line.

And that's when we discovered the order form "bump." We found that by adding a small box on the order form AFTER someone fills in their credit card information, but BEFORE they click on the submit button worked miracles. The small box offered to add the thirty-seven dollar product on to the order. We wound up with an average of about 34% of our customers adding the thirty-seven dollar product to their order!

This meant that by using a free-plus-shipping offer, we immediately got three times as many customers, and by adding the thirty-seven dollar order form bump offer, we were also able to get about one out of every three people to also order the more expensive frontend product. This new tactic gave us almost the EXACT same frontend revenue, but it brought three times more people through our upsell flow.

This little secret has allowed us to spend more than our competitors in almost every market we've ever entered. Even if you don't use a free-plus-shipping offer on your frontend (and I think you're crazy if you don't), adding this order form bump to every order form will dramatically increase your cart value with almost zero effort.

DOTCOMSECRETS LABS

Fig 13.2: This is a real example of a free-plus-shipping offer we made on my book *108 Proven Split Test Winners*.

Let's look at a real-world example of the free-plus-shipping principles in action. On the page shown in figure 13.2, people can get a free physical book titled *108 Proven Split Test Winners*. It's one of the best products I've ever created, and I was originally going to charge $997 for it. But after fighting with myself for a few weeks, I finally decided to follow my own advice. Instead of charging the amount I thought it was worth, I resolved to get it into the hands of as many people as possible. So I made it a free-plus-shipping offer. I knew when I created it that anyone who got this product in their hands would be a raving Russell Brunson fan for the rest of their life and would want to ascend my Value Ladder. On the order form we added a "bump" for our Conversion Krusher template for just thirty-seven dollars. Then after someone purchased the book, our first upsell was our Instant Traffic Hacks product for $197, our second upsell was my Perfect Webinar product for $297, and our last upsell was my High-Ticket Secrets program for $997. We started to drive traffic to "sell" my free book, and the results that came back were amazing. For each free book we gave away, we averaged about sixty-six dollars in *immediate* revenue from the upsells!

With numbers like that, just think how much more I can spend to acquire customers. And once we acquire someone as a customer, we continue to lead them up our Value Ladder to other products and services. So the revenue only continues to grow.

HOW DOES THIS WORK IF YOU'RE AN . . .

Author, Coach, or Consultant: Think of the most amazing results you could get for your clients, the one thing that would really solve their biggest problem, and put the information into a book, CD, or DVD. You may hesitate and feel some resistance to this suggestion. Many people think, *Oh no, I can't give that away . . . it's my secret sauce!* Trust me. Give it away for free, and you'll reap the benefits on the backend.

eCommerce Business: Tailor this concept to your space. For example, if you're selling something like birdcages, you could give away a CD titled *How to Teach Your Parrot to Talk*. Or, maybe you sell custom suits; you could offer free cuff links. See how this works?

Network Marketer: For this niche, you could create a CD or DVD showing your secret method of finding leads or converting them into distributors. You can then use this bait to attract people who are already interested in network marketing and who you know will make great distributors for your team.

Affiliate Marketer: Create your own informational CD or DVD to give away and build your own list and then sell other people's offers on the backend. You can even interview someone with more knowledge about the industry for your free-plus-shipping offer.

Offline Business Owner: Think about your business and the problems you help to solve. Figure out the biggest problem for your potential customers and share your unique solution. Record that solution on a CD or DVD and give it away as a free-plus-shipping offer. Or find a physical product you can offer for free-plus-shipping—anything that will attract consumers and get buyers into your Value Ladder.

Let's Review: The secret to converting cold traffic is leveraging the power of free. Whatever you're sharing in your free-plus-shipping offer, it can't be boring, general knowledge. It has to be unique, sexy, or fun—the more unique, the better. Using free-plus-shipping offers is the fastest way to qualify your buyers and get people into your Value Ladder. Remember, if someone isn't willing to pull out a credit card and pay a few bucks for shipping on your product, then they probably aren't going to buy your other products either.

Up Next: Now that we've covered all the strategy behind Value Ladders and how to turn those into sales funnels, would you like to see the seven core sales funnels we use in our companies, as well as the exact scripts we use to sell each of those products? In the next section, I will be revealing the nuts and bolts behind building your winning campaigns.

SECTION FOUR:
FUNNELS
AND SCRIPTS

IMPORTANT NOTE

Before we start this section, I want to point out that each of these funnels, and their accompanying scripts, serve a different purpose. I use all of them at different points in our company and at different levels of our Value Ladder. I also want to mention that both the sales funnels and the scripts are just a framework that form a starting point. Once we get the basic framework of a funnel working, we add on other components to grow it into a larger, more complete sales funnel. For example, for the Free-Plus-Shipping Funnel I described in the last chapter, we added an order form bump as well as three upsells or one-time offers (OTOs) to build the final funnel.

The scripts I'm giving you in this section are also just a framework. You need to add in your personality, the elements of your Attractive Character that will make these static scripts come to life. So use these funnels and scripts as the starting point, but don't be afraid to tweak them for your company's needs.

One of the biggest questions I get about funnels is this: *How in the world do I actually build these out so they all flow together the way they're supposed to?* I don't want the technology factor to get in the way of implementing what you've learned in this book. Each of the funnels I'm about to show you can easily be built out in ClickFunnels.com. In section 5, you will get a full tutorial on how to use ClickFunnels to build out these funnels.

FRONTEND FUNNELS

FUNNEL #1:

TWO-STEP, FREE-PLUS-SHIPPING

The Two-Step Funnel works really well for the free-plus-shipping offers we discussed earlier. The first page typically has a video using the Who, What, Why, How script you'll see below. Then the page asks visitors, *"Where should I ship this?"* They fill out the shipping address form (that's step one) and then move on to step two where they fill in credit card information for the shipping and handling charge. It's important that you mention on the first page that the buyers will be charged for shipping and handling. Otherwise, it's very unethical, and you'll upset your customers before they even have a chance to get into your Value Ladder, which is never a good idea. As we mentioned before, adding an order form bump on step two is a great way to increase frontend revenues. Now, not everyone who fills out step one will fill out step two, so I capture the email address on the first step. That way, I can follow up with them later and ask them to go back and fill out the rest of the form.

After the visitors fill out the second step and click the submit button, you take them to a special, one-time offer (OTO), which presents an opportunity to upgrade the order. I'll explain the psychology behind how to structure your offer for the OTOs when I share with you the sales script we use. Figure 14.1 shows one OTO, but often we'll have two or three upsells and downsells in our funnels, so you don't have to limit yourself to just one additional offer.

The psychology behind this funnel is amazing. People are more likely to fill out the first step because they don't see a long form asking for credit card information. Then once they do get to the credit card form, they keep filling it out because their brains are already committed to the process. Interestingly, I often find conversions to be higher on step one than on a regular email squeeze page, even though I'm asking for an entire shipping address instead of just a short email. This is probably because receiving something physical in the mail has a higher perceived value than receiving digital information via email.

You can see a live example at www.DotComSecretsLabs.com.

THE WHO, WHAT, WHY, HOW SCRIPT

This is the script I typically use with the Two-Step Funnel. Inexpensive offers like free-plus-shipping items usually don't require a long, involved sales letter. You need to hit the main selling points and build credibility as quickly as you can. Just create a little video, answering these four questions, and maybe add in a text version on the page. Present step one on the order form, and you're all set. This is a short and simple script that answers the main questions likely on the prospects' minds as they look at a low-end offer.

Who: Who are you? Introduce yourself very briefly.

"Hi, I'm Russell Brunson, founder of DotComSecrets."

What: What do you have? Introduce your product or offer briefly.

"I've got a free DVD that's going to show you _____."

Why: Why do they need it? Explain the benefits of the offer.

"If you've been struggling with _____, then you need this DVD because it will _____."

How: How can they get it? Walk them through the order process so they know what to expect.

"Just fill out the form on the side of this page. Let me know your shipping address, and I'll send it out right away."

The Catch: Tell them why you're offering this product for such a low price. People always think there's a catch. So instead of avoiding the topic, let them know, in clear terms, that there is no catch.

"There's no catch. I'm doing this because _____. All I need for you to do is to help with shipping and handling charges."

Urgency: Explain why they should order this product right now.

"I only have a very limited number of copies, so don't be left behind."

"This offer ends at midnight on _____. Don't wait."

Guarantee: Reverse any risk in ordering the product.

"If you don't love it, I'll refund your money, and you can keep the DVD."

Recap: Remind them what they are getting and why.

"One more time, here's what you're getting: _____."

Let's Review: The Two-Step Funnel is great for converting cold traffic and getting a visitor to qualify as a subscriber and buyer. The sales process is short and sweet because you're selling something at the low end of your Value Ladder.

Up Next: Now, after they have made the initial purchase, use a different script to sell the special, one-time offer. Let's look at that script now.

THE OTO SCRIPT

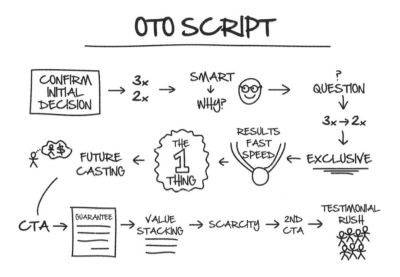

OTO stands for One Time Offer. It's a special offer you make to people who just purchased a product from you. We use this script for the OTO on all of our offers (not just the Two-Step Funnel), so know that you can and should use this script for any upsell situation. In the past, I would try to use a longer sales process in the OTO, but I never had great conversions with the longer version. It wasn't until my team wrote our script so that the focus is more on confirming the initial purchase and then quickly convincing them to say the second yes that we saw dramatically better results. Usually this OTO video is only three to five minutes long, yet it will close people on price points from ninety-seven dollars to two thousand or more.

Now, one of the keys you need to understand before you use this script is how to structure your OTO. Getting the second yes is 80% offer structure and 20% script. So here are a few guidelines to make sure you structure the offer correctly.

Rule #1: Don't Sell More of the Same Thing. This is the biggest mistake most entrepreneurs make when it comes to upsells. They try to sell more of what the customer just bought. Instead, if the customer bought an ebook titled *How to Lose Weight by Juicing*, your next offer shouldn't be another juicing product. In the visitor's mind, he has already scratched that itch, so offering more of the same rarely works.

Rule #2: Don't Sell a Random Product. The next worst thing to selling more of the same is to sell a random, unrelated product. I see this all the time. Yet, if there is no logical connection between the frontend product and the upsells, you will kill your conversions. Rather, structure your upsell offer in one of these three ways:

Sample Structure #1: The Next Thing. This is my favorite way to do upsells. If a guy just purchased your book, *How to Lose Weight by Juicing*, what is the next logical product he needs to buy from you to reach his goals? He just secured a way to learn how to juice (so that itch is scratched). But remember that he is juicing to lose weight. So, outside of juicing, what else will help him to accomplish his weight-loss goal? Is it a weight-training manual? Would he be interested in a cardio-related product? Those types of offers will convert well because it's the next thing the new customer needs in order to accomplish his core goal. This is what my team did on the backend of our *DotComSecrets Labs* book. The frontend product sold conversion secrets to a buyer obviously interested in Internet sales, so the two upsells were related to traffic and then sales.

Sample Structure #2: Do It Faster. If you have a way, a tool, a technique, or a software program that complements the initial offer and helps the customer get results faster, then the "Do-It-Faster" upsell is the right type of offer. The one key point to remember is you do NOT want to say the initial program won't work without this upsell. There is no better way to upset your new customers than to tell them that what they just bought from you is incomplete without buying more.

Sample Structure #3: Need Help? This type of upsell pushes people farther up your Value Ladder to your high-end offers. It presents a way to get specially tailored insight from you. Here we are asking the buyers if they want help implementing what they just purchased on the frontend.

Now that you understand proven ways to structure the upsell, let me show you how to use the OTO script. Below is a pattern of dialogue you can use to create your own OTO script. While you should tweak the language to match your individual offer, try to follow the order I have provided. I already organized the crucial elements for you, start to finish.

Confirm Initial Decision: It's important to put any possible buyer's remorse to rest by reinforcing the decision to purchase the initial offer. It's also important to make sure you keep an "open loop" at this stage. We used to say things like, "Congratulations, your order is complete," before we made the upsell offer, but this language closed the sales loop. The prospect's brain was thinking, *I'm finished*, and it was hard to get that second conversion. But once we changed that language to, "Wait! Your order is not yet complete," the sales loop remained open, and our conversions went up. Why? Because subconsciously the reader was still open to being sold on something else. Pretty cool, huh?

Congratulations on purchasing _____. Your order is not quite finished yet.

Smart => Why: Tell the buyer he's made a great decision by making the first purchase and why.

You've made a smart choice, and here's why . . .

You ordered this because you wanted _____, and that's exactly what it's going to do for you.

3x 2x Question: Ask the buyer if he'd like to speed up his results.

How would you like to get three times the results, twice as fast?

How would you like to get _____ (results) in _____ (time: days or weeks)?

Exclusive: Explain why this OTO is not for everyone.

This offer is NOT for everyone. We're only making it available to you because you proved you're an action taker when you took advantage of _____ (initial offer). So I'm going to make you a special, one-time offer that's only available right here, right now.

Results, Fast, Speed: Explain that this OTO will complement the original purchase by delivering better results, faster.

What I'm going to share with you right now will help you to get the results (fill in the results the customer is wanting) you're wanting in half the time.

The One Thing: Here you need to find the One Thing in your product that is the key to the buyer's success. This part is often tricky because it is tempting to explain everything about the offer. But if you do that, you will kill the sale. You need to figure out the One Thing that is the *most* valuable and will yield the best results. For example, in my OTO selling my "Perfect Webinar" system, I have over twenty-four hours of videos. But instead of telling the buyers everything they will learn, I focus on one thing, a special close the video demonstrates called "The Stack." I explain what it is, how much money it has made me, my results, and what type of results the buyer can expect from this "One Thing."

I have another product called _____. I don't have time to go over everything inside of the product because we could be here for hours, but one of the strategies inside that will give you the results you're looking for FAST is _____. Let me explain to you what it is and how it can help you. (Insert explanation.) And that is just ONE of the things that you'll learn with this product.

Future Pacing: Help the buyer imagine achieving goals faster and with greater ease.

Can you imagine what your life will be like when you have _____ (the One Thing)?

Call to Action (CTA): Tell the buyer how to order the special offer.

So click the button below right now to add _____ to your order.

Guarantee: Reverse the risk he may be feeling with a guarantee.

I guarantee _____ or _____.

Value Stacking: Add in valuable bonuses. Here's a trick for creating bonuses: take the most valuable part of your product—the thing people want MOST—pull it out, and offer it as a free bonus. People can't resist getting the thing they want most of all for "free."

If you act now, you'll also receive _____, (worth $_____), for FREE.

And _____, (worth $_____), for FREE. And _____, (worth $_____), for FREE . . .

Scarcity: Give them a reason to order right now! Make this a truly one-time offer.

This _____ (product name) is available on my website for _____ (higher price). But right now, you have this ONE CHANCE to get it for only _____. This one-time offer is only available right here, right now. When you leave this page, it's gone forever.

Second CTA: Repeat your call to action.

Don't miss your chance to _____ faster and easier than ever. Click the button now.

Testimonial Rush: Add in testimonials about your product—more is better.

Don't just take my word for it, take a look at what others are saying . . .

That's the framework for the OTO script. Now, just like the other scripts, this is a guide to show you the path you need to lead your customers down to put them in a state where they will purchase. You have some freedom to add in your own personality. Remember, your Attractive Character is essential to making these scripts come to life. So use the script as a guide, but insert your own personality for maximum conversions.

SELF-LIQUIDATING OFFER

SELF LIQUIDATING OFFER (SLO) FUNNEL

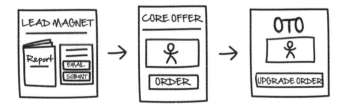

Typically, we use the Self-Liquidating Offer (SLO) Funnel when we are trying to sell a product that's priced anywhere from twenty-seven to ninety-seven dollars. The main goal is to have this frontend product cover the expenses of buying traffic. You hope to break even. That is why we call it a "self-liquidating offer"— because if you structure it right, you won't have any traffic costs, and your upsells become pure profit. In general, a free-plus-shipping offer will lose money on the frontend offer, but will use the upsells to break even or even make a profit. In contrast, SLOs should break even before any upsells.

First, you're going to attract people with a free video, report, ebook, or other lead magnet on your squeeze page. Typically, my "bribe" to get them to give me an email address is something that I'm going to show them on the next page in a video or a sales letter. Then, once the visitors subscribe to your list, they land on your SLO page, which sells your core offer. This is generally a video or a long-form-text sales letter, presenting your SLO using the Star, Story, Solution script described below. Because the price point is so much higher than a free-plus-shipping offer, you normally have to use a longer script to get your visitors comfortable enough to make a purchasing decision. That is what the Star, Story, Solution script does. On the order form, you can add an order form "bump," and then take them into your OTO sequence using the same OTO script I gave you earlier.

I love the Star, Story, Solution script because it helps to introduce your new visitors to your Attractive Character while you are selling them your product.

STAR, STORY, SOLUTION SCRIPT

I didn't invent the concept of the Star, Story, Solution script. I first heard it when I was interviewing a guy who had made one hundred million

STAR, STORY, SOLUTION

dollars in twenty-three months selling supplements. He said there was a script he used to sell all of his products. The script formula was so simple! First, you need a star (I call this person the Attractive Character), then you need a story that agitates a problem, and finally you need to provide a solution (your product).

I thought it was a powerful format, but it took me almost ten years to figure out how to frame each section of the script. After I figured out how to lead a prospect through each section, I was able to build out a framework that my companies (as well as hundreds of our clients) use over and over again.

Sometimes it's easy to feel overwhelmed with all the pieces in this script—there are forty-four! But take it one piece at a time, and you'll be fine. Each piece can be as short as a sentence or two, while others might be longer as you find places to interject your true stories, which define the Attractive Character. Just think of the forty-four pieces as stepping-stones along the path to the sale. You can write as much—or as little—as you like for each piece. If you follow the script, you'll have a great sales letter by the time you get to the end. Let's go through the scripts for all three sections: star, story, and solution.

SECTION 1: STAR

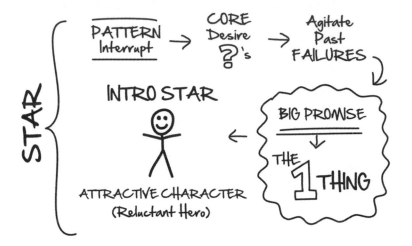

1. Pattern Interrupt: This is usually the first thing prospects see. It's important to grab their attention, get them out of their current environment or activity, and suck them into your sales copy. This isn't always easy to do! But using a pattern interrupt helps. Here's an example of a successful pattern interrupt we used for our pornography addiction product:

> *It happened again, didn't it? To you . . . or someone you love.*
>
> *I know your story . . .*
>
> *Everyone's situation is different, but the results are usually the same . . .*

Often the "core-desire questions" in step two can also work as my pattern interrupt. I've seen a lot of people who will start their sales videos showing a strange picture of an unusual object, and then say something like the following:

> *"What does this strange turtle have to do with your ____? I'm going to show you in this video, but first . . ."*

2. Core-Desire Questions: Through a series of questions, you get prospects thinking about the things they desire most. These questions move the brain to the topic you want to discuss, which is the outcome or results they wish they could achieve. Here's an example of core-desire questions from one of my ListHacking products:

I've got a quick question for you . . .

Have you ever wanted to work from home?

Own your own business?

Come on . . . you know you want that lifestyle . . . the one that everyone talks about . . .

Where you can work from home in your underwear . . .

Or on a beach with your laptop . . .

3. Agitate Past Failures: If prospects are taking the time to read your sales letter, chances are pretty good that this isn't the first time they've thought about solving this problem. If they already had the desired results, they wouldn't be searching online or clicking ads for your product, would they? So, you already know they've probably tried to achieve the result and failed. This part of the sales letter agitates that failure in their brains. Here's an example:

So . . . why hasn't it happened for you yet?

Come on . . . admit it.

This isn't the first time you've been looking for a proven way to make money . . . is it?

When is it your turn?

4. Big Promise/the One Thing: Here's where you introduce your big promise, the One Thing you're going to focus on for the rest of the sales letter.

When you watch this video to the end, you're going to discover

_____.

5. Introduce the Star: Right after you introduce your big promise, you want to introduce the star of the story. The star is the Attractive Character. I usually use the reluctant hero persona as my Attractive Character's identity. But remember you can use the leader, the adventurer, the reporter, or any other archetype you think works for your product and your market.

Hey, my name is Russell. And a few years ago, I was just like you . . .

SECTION 2: STORY

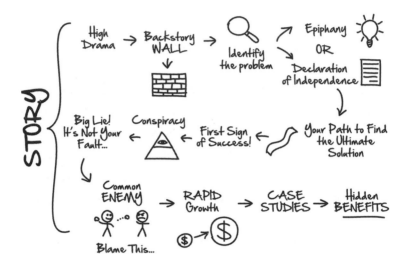

Now it's time to transition into the second section of the sales letter, your Attractive Character's story. If you've already written your Soap Opera Sequence, this section will seem very familiar.

6. High Drama: Whenever you're telling a story, you want to start at the point of high drama. Don't start with, "Well, I woke up and had eggs for breakfast . . . then I got dressed and went to work . . . blah, blah, blah." Do start with, "The gun was in my face. I was staring down the dark barrel, and I could see the bullet in the chamber. My heart pounded in my ears, and rivers of sweat streamed down my face . . ."

Think about your favorite movies. Do they start at the very beginning of the story, way before the main event occurs? Probably not.

A good movie, like a good story, starts at the point of high drama. The same works for your sales letters. Present your Attractive Character at a moment that is powerful, dramatic, and compelling:

I crawled out from under my desk, almost hitting my head as I grabbed the phone . . .

"Hello," I muttered.

"WHAT THE #@%#^$@ ARE YOU DOING!?" responded the stranger on the other line.

Confused, I asked him what he was talking about.

"In the past six hours, we have received over thirty spam complaints from YOUR IP address . . . Russell, you're a SPAMMER, and we're shutting off your Internet access."

"What!?"

I was so confused . . .

I got a lump in my stomach as I hung up the phone and realized that I now had to explain to my new wife of just six weeks that I'm the reason our Internet is shut off.

7. Backstory WALL: Next you want to fill in the backstory that led up to the point of high drama. How did you, or your Attractive Character, get there? It's important that the featured character eventually hit a wall, a point where he was completely stuck. This, by the way, is where your prospects probably are right now. They have likely tried to make money online or lose weight or get whatever result you're promising, but they can't seem to get the result they want. It feels hopeless.

You see, just six hours earlier, I had "officially" started my new business as an email marketer . . .

Or so I thought . . .

I had been trying to learn online marketing for almost a year now, and I kept hearing people talk about how the MOST IMPORTANT thing you can have is . . .

Your own email list.

It made total sense to me.

I did the math. If I had ten thousand people on my email list, and I was selling a five-dollar product, then I ONLY had to get 1% of them to buy . . .

In order to make five thousand dollars . . . (1% of 10,000 was 1,000 people x $5 = $5K)

It made total sense . . . right?

And I saw others doing it. All I needed was an email list.

I just had no idea how to get one . . .

8. Identify the Problem: Now reveal the problem. Let them know why your Attractive Character was stuck (which is also probably the reason they are currently stuck). In fact, the more closely you can relate your Attractive Character's problem to the readers' problems, the better.

The problem I had was _____.

9. Epiphany OR Declaration of Independence: Once the AC pinpoints the problem, it's usually not long before they have an epiphany or decide to make a major change in their behavior or mindset. For example, your Attractive Character might have an epiphany that to make money online, he has to build a list. Or in order to lose weight, he has to change his eating behavior once and for all.

And that's when I had my big "Ah-ha" moment . . .

That's when I decided I HAD to make a change.

10. Your Path to Finding the Ultimate Solution: Take the reader along your journey. Describe some of the different things you, or your AC, tried before you found success.

So, first I tried _____. That didn't work at all.

Then I tried _____, and it was a little better . . .

11. First Sign of Success: Let the reader see you start to succeed. Some of your prospects might be experiencing this feeling at the moment; they might be right on the cusp of early success. You want them to see you go through this step so that they know you've moved through it to the ultimate success, and they can, too.

And that's when I finally tried _____. And guess what? This time it worked!

12. Conspiracy: Show them how you finally realized that the cards were stacked against you from the start. Your prospects are probably convinced that the cards are currently stacked against them. Because they believe it, you need to address this fear through the Attractive Character's story.

And that's when I realized it wasn't my fault! It's because of _____. No wonder I was struggling!

13. The Big Lie: Explain why it's not their fault that they haven't succeeded before now.

For years, they had been telling me _____, and when I figured out that it wasn't true, I was finally able to break out of their chains and get the results I deserved.

14. Common Enemy: This is who or what is really to blame for the big lie that was holding the AC back and blocking his success.

The real problem is _____. They were the ones keeping me from _____.

15. Rapid Growth: Now show them how fast the AC progressed once he realized the truth.

Once I realized _____, that's when we started to _____ really FAST!

16. Case Studies: Highlight the stories of others who've had success similar to your or the Attractive Character's story.

But it wasn't just me. Take a look at what _____ has done for others.

17. Hidden Benefits: Explain the benefits you didn't expect that have resulted from the product/discovery you are describing to the reader.

*I didn't realize when I started that not only does it _____,
but it also _____, _____, and _____.*

SECTION 3: SOLUTION

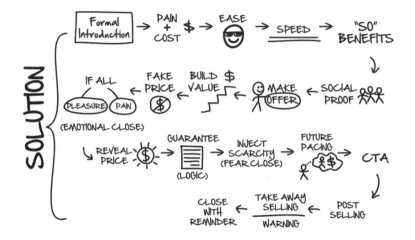

Now it's time to bring it all together and wrap up your pitch in a nice, neat package (that the readers can buy).

18. Formal Introduction: Introduce the product.

And that's why I created _____.

19. Pain and Cost: Tell them what you had to go through to create the product.

This took _____ (time) to create, and cost me _____. But it was totally worth it.

20. Ease: How much effort does the product save you?

It makes _____ so much easier!

21. Speed: How much time does the product save you?

What used to take me _____ (time), I can get done in _____ (time).

22. "So" Benefits: Explain why they need this by writing out three or four benefits followed by the words "so _____."

*Burns fat while you sleep, **so** you can lose weight without exercising.*

*Builds your list on autopilot, **so** you can concentrate on running your business.*

23. Social Proof: These are your testimonials. Let the prospects read what others say about the product.

But don't just take my word for it. Here's what others are saying:

"This _____ saves me time and effort every day! I love how it _____ and _____."

24. Make the Offer: Explain what the buyers will get.

But, before you get started, let me ask you a question . . .

Would you like to get access to _____?

For less than the cost of a cheap meal for two, you can get access to everything inside of _____.

Now, while it would be impossible to show you ALL of the benefits of _____, I want to show you some of the things that you'll experience as soon as you're on the inside.

25. Build Value: Add bonuses and additional features, but be sure they support the "One Thing," the focus of your entire sales letter.

Plus, you'll get _____, _____, and _____.

26. Float a Fake Price: Tell the readers how much the product "should" be worth if they had to pay for each item separately. It should be a number much higher than the actual price, but you must also make sure the product really is worth the price you name. Be ethical. Explain why the high price is justified, based on its value.

The total value of all this is _____ because _____.

27. Emotional Close (If/All): Use the words *"If all . . ."* to help anchor the offer and help the buyers justify the fake price you named earlier. Use both "toward pleasure" and "away from pain" statements.

If all this did was give you the house of your dreams, would it be worth it? (Toward pleasure.)

If all this did was let you fire your boss, would it be worth it? (Away from pain.)

28. Reveal the Real Price: Now tell the readers how much they are actually going to pay. This price should be much lower than the high price you floated earlier.

I'm not going to charge you _____. I'm only going to charge you _____.

29. Guarantee (Logic): Reverse any risk the potential buyers may be feeling. Give the guarantee some crazy name.

I'm going to take on all the risk, and give you my _____ (crazy name) guarantee.

30. Inject Scarcity (Fear Close): Give the buyers a legitimate reason to buy NOW.

But you must act now because _____.

31. Future Pacing: Help them see how awesome their lives are about to become—after they buy your product.

Just imagine what life will be like when _____.

32. Call to Action: Tell them what to do to make a purchase. Also, tell the prospects what's going to happen next.

So click on the button below right now, and you'll be taken to a secure order form. After you put in your credit card information, you'll be taken to a secure members' area where you can download _____, even if it's 2:00 a.m.!

33. Post Selling: Make the readers feel like they might be left behind if they don't hurry.

For those who are already signing up, this is what's going to happen next . . .

34. Take Away Selling (Warning): Explain that they need to make a decision, and it doesn't matter to you whether they order or not.

You see . . . it doesn't matter to us if you sign up right now or not.

We'll still be going about our daily business and hitting our financial goals with absolute certainty—whether you join our team or not.

However, without our help, you'll ALWAYS be working harder than you really need to.

I know it sounds kind of harsh, but I think you'll agree that it's true.

35. Close with Reminder: This is a summary for the skimmers, but it can remind all readers of the offer.

Remember, you get _____ (recap the offer).

That's it. The entire script for a long-form Star, Story, Solution sales letter. It works great for both text and video sales letters. Don't forget, you need to infuse each of the steps with the personality of the Attractive Character. Use these forty-four pieces as a framework to get you from the opening lines to the sale.

FUNNEL #3:

CONTINUITY

CONTINUITY FUNNEL

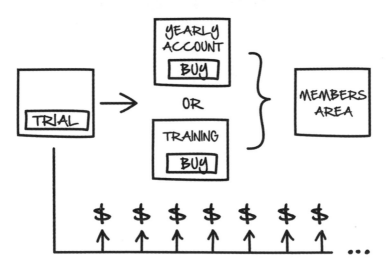

The last type of frontend funnel that I want to show you is our Continuity Funnel. One of my mentors, David Frey, said (and I wholeheartedly agree) that if you don't have continuity, then you don't have a business. In every business, there are ways to add continuity income, and it's an essential part of every Value Ladder. Continuity is when you get paid regularly, usually every month, for ongoing access to information or software or some other product.

The funnel itself is very simple. Once a visitor has moved through either a Two-Step or an SLO Funnel and made it through my Soap Opera Sequence, then I will usually send them through a short email sequence promoting my Continuity Funnel. Once people are in the program, they are charged on a regular basis for continuing. Usually, this is a monthly charge, but it could also be weekly, or yearly.

Many people ask me where they should use Continuity Funnels. You can use them as a frontend to generate leads (and we do this with some of our Continuity Funnels), but I prefer to use them as the second funnel in my sequence—after my customers have had a chance to bond with the Attractive Character. Waiting dramatically increases our stick rate (how long the customer remains an active, paying member).

Now, one exciting thing about this funnel is you are able to use the same scripts that we have already introduced to get people to join your continuity programs.

If you are selling a free or one-dollar trial, then the Who, What, Why, How script typically works the best. We've also had incredible success adding in order form bumps that give our customers training on how to use the continuity program. If you are planning on selling continuity without a trial, then I would recommend using the Star, Story, Solution script.

After people have purchased the membership, you can create OTOs like we discussed earlier. We have found yearly or lifetime accounts to be incredibly effective upsells with continuity programs.

FUNNELS FOR THE MIDDLE
OF THE VALUE LADDER

FUNNEL #4:

THE PERFECT WEBINAR

SALES WEBINAR FUNNEL

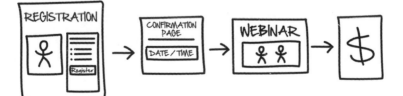

Webinars have become extremely popular sales tools over the past few years, mainly because they work so well. They take the old teleseminar/speaking model to a whole new level. Back when I was doing a lot of speaking from the stage, my main income came from all the products and coaching I sold after a presentation was over. This is called "back of the room" selling because there was always a table set up at the back of the room where participants could go to buy whatever product I was promoting. That model works really well, but your sales are limited by the number of participants in the room. There may be hundreds or thousands of people who would love to buy your product, but for whatever reason, they aren't at that seminar. Webinars change that dynamic completely. With a webinar, you can deliver your presentation online. People don't have to travel anywhere to catch your speech (and you don't have to travel anywhere either).

At its most basic level, a webinar is nothing more than a PowerPoint presentation that you broadcast live (or record) over the Internet. It allows you to give your sales presentation to just about anyone in any corner of the globe. The best part is you can record the webinar once and then broadcast it over and over again. This is called an "automated webinar," and it's made me a fortune over the years. Webinars can be as long as you want. In fact, you'll learn about the Invisible Funnel Webinar in the next chapter—that one can be as long as four hours! The Perfect Webinar we're discussing in this chapter typically runs for about sixty to ninety minutes.

There are two parts to most webinars: the content and the sales pitch. Occasionally, you may want to give an all-content webinar, but for the most part, you'll be selling something at the end of your presentation. You promise to teach people something on the webinar. Then, if they want to learn more or dive deeper into the topic, they can purchase your product or sign up for coaching (or whatever you're selling). It's very important that the content of the webinar is valuable on its own, but as you'll see from the Perfect Webinar script, you can craft the material in a way that also helps to set up the sale. In this chapter, we're going to cover the sales funnels for both a one-time webinar and also for automated (or evergreen) webinar.

SALES WEBINAR FUNNEL

The funnel for a sales webinar is very simple. You drive traffic to a registration page where you have some sort of sales letter or video encouraging readers to sign up for the webinar. Typically I use the Who, What, Why, How script on my webinar registration pages. After watching the video or reading the copy, the interested prospects fill in their name and email to register. (Boom! They're now on your list.) Then you send them to a confirmation page where they are reminded of the date and time of the webinar and given instructions on how to call in. At the appointed time, they will attend the webinar, and you can sell them your product. Often people can't make it to the live webinar for some reason. So you may decide to send a recording. After all, the more people who hear your pitch, the more products you're likely to sell.

AUTOMATED WEBINAR FUNNEL

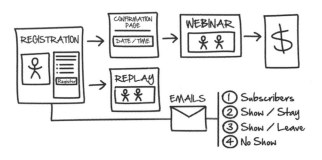

Typically I will do a webinar live once, and then I take the recording from that event and build out an Automated Webinar Funnel that will allow me to keep sending traffic to that website every day for the rest of my life. It's nice because you can keep selling your products twenty-four hours a day, seven days a week, in every country in the world! At the time of this writing, I currently have two webinars that have both made me over a million dollars. Both are still selling to people right now while I'm writing this book!

We add a few extra steps to the regular Sales Webinar Funnel to make this one run continuously. You start by driving traffic to a registration page that uses the Who, What, Why, How script, and people enter their names and emails to register. Then they go to a confirmation page where they get the date and time, set for some point in the future, or they can choose to watch "yesterday's" replay right away.

The webinar itself is the same format as the regular sales webinar; we deliver content and sell something at the end. (In a few pages, I'll give you the Perfect Webinar script, which will show you exactly how to do this.)

My team carefully tracks when a participant leaves, and then we send out a different email sequence, depending on how long they watched. Everyone who subscribes gets one sequence. Everyone who shows up and stays all the way to the end gets another sequence. People who show up but leave early get yet another sequence. And the no-shows get an entirely different sequence to encourage them to go back and watch a replay. Each sequence encourages people to either go back and finish watching, or go order the product we're selling. Once the participant places an order, the email sequences should stop automatically.

THE PERFECT WEBINAR SCRIPT

Now that you have people signed up, what are you going to say? How you structure your webinar has everything to do with how much you sell at the end.

A typical webinar is broken down into three sections: the introduction, the content, and the close (or the sales pitch). Over the past ten years, I've had a chance to speak and sell on stages all around the world, and I've had the chance to learn from some of the best stage closers in the world. This script incorporates strategies I learned from at least a dozen different people. It's the outline I now use for every webinar, and it works.

There are a lot of pieces to this script, but try not to get overwhelmed. Think of it as just three sections—introduction, content, and the stack— then fill those three sections in with the scripts provided.

INTRODUCTION: This should take about five minutes. It introduces you, your subject, and your credibility.

Hi, I'm Russell Brunson, founder of DotComSecrets and CEO of several multi-million-dollar companies.

Big Promise: Repeat your big promise. This is the One Thing that got the participants to sign up in the first place. It's also the ruler they will use to judge your webinar's quality. If you don't set this ruler, then they will measure the value of your webinar based on something outside of your control.

In the next sixty minutes, you are going to learn my exact strategy on "how to _____, without _____."

Hook to End: Give the participants a reason to stick around all the way to the end of the webinar. Free giveaways are popular. You could also promise to do something funny or show them something cool.

Don't forget! At the end of the webinar, I'm going to give you a secret link where you can download a transcript of everything I'm going to show you today. You have to be watching live in order to get this, so stick around. I promise it will be worth your time.

Command Attention: Tell them to close out of Facebook, turn off their cell phones, and give you their undivided attention. Also, you might ask the participants to grab a pen and paper for taking notes.

I know there are distractions all around us, but this strategy I'm about to share can change your life. I don't want you to miss a single crucial step. So, please . . . make a commitment to stay focused. Can you do that for yourself? Close out of Facebook. Stop checking your email. Turn off your cell phone. Give me your complete attention.

Qualify Yourself: Let the participants know why you are qualified to speak on the subject.

You're probably wondering why I'm qualified to teach on this topic. Here's my story: _____.

Future Pace: Lead the viewers through some imagination exercises where they can picture what life could be like once they learn the secrets you're about to reveal. Be descriptive and appeal to all five senses, if possible.

Imagine what your life will be like after you know how to

_____.

Can you see _____? *Would that make things better for you?*

THE CONTENT: This is the meat of the webinar. It should run about fifty to sixty minutes, and it should deliver whatever content you promised in the registration script. I like to focus on one main idea and then reveal three secrets about that One Thing. So, I'm really teaching three things, but they all relate to the main idea I'm selling.

The One Thing: The One Thing is the core content of this webinar. It's the reason the participants showed up. What do they want or need to learn or understand? Every teaching point through the webinar must point back to THIS one thing. I always try to break down my "One Thing" into this simple format:

How to _____ without _____.

How to add high-ticket sales to your sales funnel instantly— without you personally talking to anyone on the phone . . . ever!

This is the One Thing from my High-Ticket Secrets Webinar. For this offer, I looked at what the other "gurus" were teaching about making high-ticket sales. They were all teaching how to close people on the phone. Well, I HATE talking on the phone, and I think most of my audience does, too. So, I decided to show people how they can still take advantage of the income-boosting potential of high-ticket sales *without* talking on the phone.

After I explain this big idea—the One Thing—I share three secrets that will expand on what I promised to reveal. Typically, when I'm creating these three secrets, I'm looking to debunk existing beliefs participants might have that would keep them from purchasing the product from me at the end of the webinar.

For my High-Ticket Secrets Webinar, there were three belief patterns that I had to break in order to get people to buy. Below are the common beliefs and then the secrets I created to destroy that line of thinking:

SECRET #1

Break: *The best model for making money online is to sell products.*

Rebuild: *You can make more money in one day selling high-ticket products than you can in a MONTH by selling normal products.*

SECRET #2

Break: *To sell high-ticket products, I have to sell on the phone.*

Rebuild: *You don't personally have to sell anything! (Big plus because I hate phones!) Let me show you how to build a two-person, mini call center to close all of the sales for you.*

SECRET #3

Break: *It probably costs a fortune to drive enough traffic to make this work.*

Rebuild: *You only need a little bit of traffic to make this work (about one hundred clicks a day).*

Remember, teaching these three secrets should take fifty to sixty minutes. So be sure to tell stories, show examples, and use this as an opportunity to get your audience to bond with the Attractive Character.

THE STACK: This section of the webinar should last at least ten minutes. Often, I allow for twenty minutes or more, depending on what I'm selling. The hardest part of selling on a webinar, for most people, is transitioning into the close. They start to get nervous, and the hesitation shows in the voice and confidence level. The best way I've found to transition is simply to say, *Let me ask you a question . . .,* and then you move straight into how your product will help the participants with whatever your One Thing is. Once you transition into your sales pitch, you're going to use something called "The Stack."

The Stack: I consider The Stack my secret weapon. I learned it from one of my mentors, Armand Morin. I saw him speak on stage and close nearly half the room with almost no effort. I pulled him aside to find out what he was doing, and he explained to me The Stack. I started using it immediately, and I went from closing on average 5-10% of a room to consistently closing 20% or more. Then I started using it on my sales webinars and saw a dramatic increase in how much I made with each viewing. It's worked so well and so consistently that I will never give a sales presentation again without it.

Armand taught me that the only thing your prospect remembers when you sell is the last thing you showed him. He explained that most sales presentations focus on the core offer, then a list of bonuses. So the last thing shown is the last bonus, followed by a call to action to get the prospect to buy. The problem with this is when the person doesn't think that the *last thing* you offered is worth the price. They simply won't buy under those circumstances.

So, Armand builds a presentation slide called a Stack Slide. This slide has everything included in the offer, presented in a long, bulleted list. He introduces the first bullet point, talks about it, moves to the second bullet point, and so on. But when he shows the slide with the second bullet, he re-stacks the offer:

So what that means is that you're first going to get _____ and also _____.

He then talks about the next component of the offer and reveals the next stack slide, but this time, there are three products listed in the offer, stacked from the first mentioned to the last. Be sure to notice the order and arrangement:

So what that means is that you're first going to get _____ and also _____ AND also this _____.

He keeps doing this throughout the entire close. When he gets to that last part of the offer, he shows the final stack slide, with EVERYTHING listed, and recaps everything on that slide. Then, he finally introduces the price. Now, prospects associate the price with the full offer—not just the last thing he mentions.

After you reveal your full stack slide, you want to show the total value of everything the buyers are going to receive. Even though the price you name first isn't what buyers will actually pay, you need to anchor that price in their minds before you move on. We do that by introducing "If all" statements similar to the ones we used in the Star, Story, Solution script.

If/All: Use the words "If all" to anchor the offer and help the buyer justify the price you have given. Use both "toward pleasure" and "away from pain" statements.

If all this did was give you the house of your dreams, would it be worth it? (Toward pleasure.)

If all this did was let you fire your boss, would it be worth it? (Away from pain.)

Reveal the Real Price: Now tell them the actual price. This price should be much lower than the price you gave after The Stack.

I'm not going to charge you _____. I'm only going to charge you _____.

Those are all the core elements of a Perfect Webinar. It's the path I take my customers down when I am selling them anything on a webinar. I do have a variety of ways I close out a webinar. As you can see from the image at the beginning of this chapter, there are sixteen methods that I use in most of my presentations. In order to make these clear to you, I created a special video demonstrating how to use the sixteen closes while you are doing The Stack. To see that video, go to www. DotComSecretsBook.com/resources/closes.

Now that you know the structure of the Perfect Webinar, how would you like to learn how to get people to *pay you to sell them* high-ticket offers? We've developed a special webinar funnel where people will pay you for the privilege of letting you sell them on your highest-priced offerings. And they'll do it with smiles on their faces. It's called the Invisible Funnel Webinar, and it's next!

INVISIBLE FUNNEL WEBINAR

INVISIBLE FUNNEL

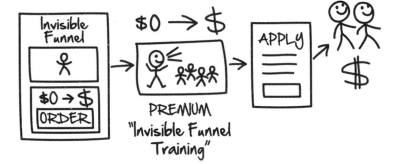

T he next way we sell products in the middle of the Value Ladder is through a concept we call the Invisible Funnel. The Invisible Funnel is a concept that was created by Daegan Smith. It's a powerful tool my team has used often over the past few years to get people to ascend our Value Ladder quickly.

The Invisible Funnel is a premium webinar that people pay for AFTER the webinar is over—if (and only if) they love what you taught them. Let's look at how it works.

We drive traffic to a website that uses The Magic Bullet script to get people to sign up for the Invisible Funnel-style webinar. To register, participants enter their credit card details, but they are not billed anything right then. They watch the webinar, which is usually three or four hours of amazing, high-value content. Then, AFTER the webinar is over, *if* they agree that the webinar was worth the pre-determined price, then they do nothing, and you charge the card the next day. If the participants don't think the webinar was worth the money, they must send you an email before a certain deadline so that you won't charge their card. This format lets people try before they buy, and it gives you a chance to show off your very best content first.

At the end of the webinar, you can do a very soft sale to push the participants to an application page where they can upgrade to your high-ticket backend products or services. If you structure your Invisible Funnel correctly, you'll find that it's a really cool way to get people to buy things—without ever *selling* them anything. It creates tons of good will and builds a strong bond with the Attractive Character.

Let's talk about the numbers from my first Invisible Funnel Webinar.

We had five hundred and fifty people register with their credit cards.

From those five hundred and fifty people, 85% of them showed up for the actual webinar. (This number was shocking, considering that roughly 30% attendance is common on free webinars.)

I taught for four hours. At the end, I told those who didn't love it to let me know, and I promised not to charge their credit cards.

From that offer, we only had about 10% of the people cancel. So we were able to bill 90% of them the forty-seven dollar price tag, totaling about $23.5K. That's not bad, considering I hadn't sold anything to anyone yet. I just gave them a bunch of cool value in the form of information.

Finally, I invited those on the webinar to apply for my high-end coaching services, and from that offer, we got a stack of applications that turned into an additional six figures in business over the next thirty days.

We've successfully used the Invisible Funnel to sell weight-loss products, dating advice, speed-reading programs, and a whole bunch more. I don't use the Invisible Funnel for every selling situation, but it's a powerful tool that my team uses a few times each year to build a ton of good will with our audience—and to make some extra money while we do it.

Let me show you exactly how to get people to register for an Invisible Funnel Webinar.

MAGIC BULLET WEBINAR REGISTRATION SCRIPT

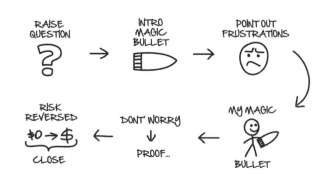

A "Magic Bullet" is simply the One Thing you're promising they'll get out of the webinar within a certain amount of time, or they don't pay. There's an old saying in direct response marketing that you have to "sell it, even if it's free." That goes for these "try before you buy" webinars, too. I do have a script that I use to get people to pull out their credit cards and sign up. For a video sales letter, this script should be somewhere between two and three minutes—not too long.

Raise the Question: Set up your Magic Bullet by asking questions that bring people's desires to the front of their minds. Make them wish they had what you're about to offer. You want the answers to the questions to be YES! Raising desire questions at the beginning of the sales letter works really well. Depending on your market, you may want to use questions that move people toward pleasure or away from pain.

Example dialogue to move the participant toward pleasure:

What if you could plug any book into your brain, instantly download that knowledge, and implement that information into your life?

Do you want to learn a new language?

Do you desire to learn how to make money?

Are you ready to score high on a test?

Example dialogue for moving a participant away from pain:

Let me ask you a question . . .

Do you ever feel like you're the only guy in the world who can't talk to a pretty girl?

Do your hands start to sweat when you walk into a room full of people?

Does your heart beat so fast it feels like it might burst out of your chest right then and there?

Does the thought of humiliation keep you home at night . . . all alone?

The final question should say something like, "Wouldn't it be nice if . . .," or "Wouldn't it be awesome if . . .".

Wouldn't it be nice if there were a way to learn anything almost instantly AND retain it all much longer?

Wouldn't it be great if you could walk into any social situation and feel totally at ease?

Wouldn't it be awesome if you could eat whatever you wanted every day and still lose weight?

Introduction: Next you want to introduce yourself and the idea of the Magic Bullet you are going to offer in the webinar training.

Hi, my name is Russell, and those are questions I used to ask myself as well.

Just imagine if you had that ability. What would you learn? What information would you want if you could instantly download it into your brain?

Point out Frustrations: Your prospects have probably tried other solutions and failed. You need to let them know their frustrations are normal, and that you once had them, too. Don't tell them what their frustrations are directly. Instead, explain *your* frustrations because they are likely the same things they are struggling with.

Unfortunately, gaining knowledge isn't as easy as inserting a socket into our brains to download the information.

We have to find a good one to two hours if we want to open a book and sit down to read. Even if we read quickly, it's going to take days to get the information we need out of the book.

While you might try using the Internet to speed up the process, you can quickly become bogged down with millions of pages of listings for any topic you want to study.

Talk about "information overload" . . .

If you've ever felt that frustration with learning a new topic, then I can relate to you perfectly.

My Magic Bullet: Now you introduce the amazing solution you're selling. Tell perspective participants about the tangible thing they're going to get by attending the webinar. If you get your Magic Bullet right, the rest of the sale is very easy. So take some time to craft the best Magic Bullet Solution your business can offer. For clarity, I try to phrase it like this: *You'll get _____ (result) by _____ (short amount of time), or you pay nothing.* The more tangible the result, the better.

You also want to describe how you discovered the solution and what the value of that solution has been to you. How did this secret change your life? What was the emotional value for you? A Magic Bullet in the dating niche might be "Get a girlfriend this weekend—or pay nothing." A weight-loss example might be something like, "Try my three-day detox and lose seven pounds, or you don't pay anything." The Magic Bullet for speed reading might be: "Double your reading speed in four hours—or pay nothing." To draw in the most participants, expand the main idea of your Magic Bullet and tell the reader a story about how this solution has worked for you:

> *Just like you, I struggled with reading—until I found the secret. I met this guy named Howard Berg at a seminar. He spent just a few short hours with me, and I was able almost INSTANTLY to double how fast I could read! I started telling my friends, family members, and business associates about what Howard did at my office; what happened next shocked me. Some people were BEGGING me to meet him so they could double their reading speed . . . Others were really skeptical that it was even possible . . .*
>
> *So I gave them a challenge . . . the SAME challenge that I'm going to give to you right now. Pay Howie one hundred dollars, and I guarantee that he'll MORE than double your reading speed in an afternoon . . . and from that point forward, for the rest of your life, you'll have a skill that will serve you forever.*

Don't Worry (Proof): Now you're going to introduce the fact that you are offering a premium webinar. You'll also tell the participants not to worry because you're going to prove its worth before you charge them any money.

And if you're skeptical . . . then don't worry. Keep the hundred dollars in your pocket, and then AFTER he's personally trained you and you've doubled your reading speed . . . then pay him the hundred.

AND . . . if he isn't able to double your reading . . . don't pay him anything. Does that seem fair? We called this the "Howard Berg, Double-Your-Speed Challenge".

And so far . . . Howard has NEVER lost. So, I set up a special webinar event this week for YOU and Howard Berg . . .

If you are on this webinar . . . Howard will double your reading speed and prove his amazing results to you . . .

Risk Reversal (0 —> $$): Here's where you offer the "try before you buy" option.

Here's what I want to do for you: I'm so sure this will completely change your life that I'm going to let you listen to the entire webinar for FREE. Then, at the end, you get to be the judge. Either I live up to my word or I don't.

If I do deliver what I promise and you love the information, do nothing and we'll charge your credit card one hundred dollars.

If I don't deliver, or you don't think the information was worth the price, just send me an email before midnight, and we won't charge you anything.

Does that sound fair?

It's kind of like going to a restaurant and only paying if you love the food.

Or going to a movie, and if you hate it . . . then you pay NOTHING . . .

The Close: Get the reader to commit to giving your webinar a try.

So, now it's your turn to decide.

Say yes, and let us prove that our system works.

You will need to put your credit card number in now to reserve your spot, but you pay NOTHING until after the webinar is over, and then pay only if you love it.

You've got nothing to lose by giving this a try.

If there's even a chance that this could completely change your life . . .isn't it worth checking it out for free?

Just click the button below, and reserve your spot for this life-changing webinar. I promise it will be worth it.

This Magic Bullet script is pretty simple, and I can usually write up one of these sales letters in less than an hour. If you follow this script, swapping out the reading program for the details of your training, you should be able to get it done quickly—even if you hate writing sales letters. This script is proven to work. Just tweak it to fit your business and your offer. And remember, once you get your Magic Bullet right, everything else should come together with ease.

Now that you've got people signed up for your webinar, what the heck do you say for two to four hours? I know providing value for that long might sound intimidating, but you can do it! Let's dive into the script I use for all our Invisible Webinars.

INVISIBLE WEBINAR CONTENT

Once you have participants signed up for your webinar, you still have some work to do. It's important to structure the webinar correctly so that all who watch feel like they've gotten their money's worth. You want each participant to be more than happy to pay you at the end. You also want to use the correct lead up and soft sales pitch for your high-ticket consulting or coaching package at the end of the webinar. Remember, this webinar is going to be three or four hours long! So you may need to bring in multiple pieces of content. Don't hold anything back. Give viewers your best stuff! Tell them everything they want to know. Answer any questions they ask. Trust me, the four hours will go by before you know it.

Here's how to structure your Invisible Funnel Webinar:

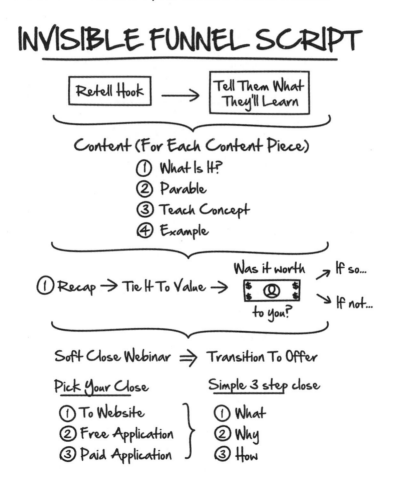

Re-tell Hook: You got the participants to register for this webinar by using your Magic Bullet script (the "try before you buy" hook), so you need to reinforce the rules they are playing by during this webinar. They get a chance to vote with their wallet at the end: did the webinar deliver or not? And remind them they must stick around until the end because only then will you give the secret email address where they can email you if they don't think the webinar was worth the price of admission.

Tell Them What They'll Learn: Give all participants an overview of the system that you are going to be teaching on this particular webinar.

Content (for each content piece): Start teaching your content now. It doesn't really matter how many pieces you teach—as long as it's your best stuff and it fills up the three or four hours you promised. You may want to practice teaching the content pieces out loud so that you know how much time to budget during the actual webinar. Here's how you want to present each content piece:

- **What Is It?** Give the content piece a cool name, making it easy to remember.
- **Parable:** Tell a memorable story to demonstrate the concept and cement it in the participant's brain.
- **Teach Concept:** Go through the nuts and bolts of the concept.
- **Example (real life, if possible):** Give some examples of how the concept works in real life. If you have case studies that show your students or clients succeeding, those are the best examples.

Recap: After you have finished teaching the content for your training, then you want to remind them again about everything they learned while they were on the training with you.

Tie It to Value: Help participants see how much this information will be worth after they implement it. After you have anchored the "true-worth" price in their minds, then you can come back to the actual asking price of this webinar. How much money will they make after they implement all they learned? How much time could they save? What's the emotional value of the knowledge they gained? Will it save them embarrassment or grief? Lay out all the benefits for them.

Was It Worth $___ to You? Ask the participant to decide whether the webinar was worth this price.

- **If so:** Do nothing, and we will bill your credit card the agreed-upon price.
- **If not:** Email us at _____ before _____, and let us know this content wasn't for you, and we won't charge your card.

Transition to Offer: Briefly mention that the participant may now want personalized help.

I know we've covered a TON of information today, and some of you are probably wishing you could get some help with setting all this up. Am I right? Quickly, I want to let you know that I do have a personal coaching program. It's not cheap because you get my personal attention the whole way through the process, but I make sure you have everything you need to be successful. Also, because I'm personally involved and work very closely with my students, I can only help a limited number of people. So, the only way to get in is to apply for a slot. You've received everything you need to succeed in this webinar, but if you are interested in getting my personal help, here's what you should do next . . .

Pick Your Close: Where will you send people to fill out an application?

- **To Website:** Give the URL where a participant can pay for your coaching.

- **Free Application:** If this is a free application, make clear that there is no charge to apply.
- **Paid Application:** If you're charging participants to apply, let them know how much and how they should pay.

Simple, Three-Step Close: This is a very soft sell. You want to let people know that you do offer personal coaching or consulting to help them get the best results as fast as possible. Then tell them where to go to fill out an application.

- **What:** Tell them what your service consists of.
- **Why:** Tell them why they should apply.
- **How:** Tell them how to apply.

Let's Review: Invisible Webinars are a great way to get people into your Value Ladder for free and build a relationship between them and the Attractive Character. Be sure to build in so much value that you can quickly ascend the viewer to your highest levels. Webinars can accomplish all this in a way that is fun for the participant. I've made hundreds of thousands of dollars using this style of teaching, and people just love it. The keys to making it work are having the right Magic Bullet (promising a result they'll get *before* they pay) and delivering what you promised.

Up Next: Do you have a new product, but aren't sure how to launch it into the world? The next chapter will show you our Product Launch Funnel and provide the scripts we use for each step.

FUNNEL #6:

PRODUCT LAUNCH

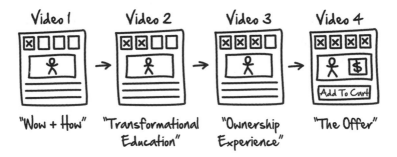

PRODUCT LAUNCH FUNNEL

Video 1	Video 2	Video 3	Video 4
"Wow + How"	"Transformational Education"	"Ownership Experience"	"The Offer"

The Product Launch Funnel was made famous by Jeff Walker, and since then, just about every Internet marketer in almost every niche has used this funnel in some way—because the approach works. Basically, you're breaking up your sales presentation over four videos—each providing a ton of value, while educating your prospects and selling your products. This funnel works best with warm and hot traffic. So, typically you're emailing your own list or an affiliate partner's list with links to the videos.

This Product Launch Funnel is broken down into four videos:

Video #1 is called "Wow and How," where you will "wow" them with a big idea, and then show them "how" you and others are using this concept.

Video #2 is the "Transformational Education" piece, where you will actually let people look over your shoulder as you walk through the process with them.

Video #3 is the "Ownership Experience" piece, where you show viewers what it's like to live when they have this in their lives.

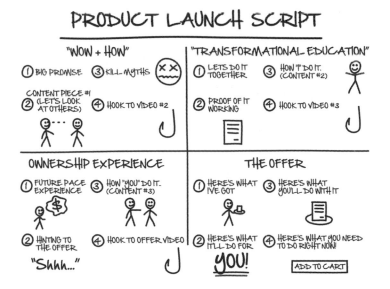

Video #4 is "The Offer," where you will reveal what you're selling, the price, and how they can get it.

Let's take a look at how each of these videos is scripted to make sales. The following scripts will show you what to say in each video. The videos can be as long as they need to be, but I find that the sweet spot is around ten to twenty minutes.

VIDEO #1: "WOW AND HOW"

Big Promise: This is your One Thing, the valuable principle you have promised to teach during these training videos.

How to sell high-ticket products without getting on the phone.

Kill Myths: Dispel any common objections or reasons the potential participant might not believe you.

You may think you have to be a sales expert and hang out on the phone all day to sell high-ticket products, but that's not true anymore. I've sold hundreds of thousands of dollars with this simple process.

Let's Look at Others (Content #1): Show how others achieve these results all the time. Tell stories and case studies.

Meet _____. She did _____, without _____.

Here's _____. He couldn't believe how easy it was to _____. Just look at his results: _____.

Hook to Video #2: Get them excited about the next video.

Tomorrow, you'll discover you can _____, even though _____.

VIDEO #2: "TRANSFORMATIONAL EDUCATION"

Let's Do It Together: It's okay if you don't think you can do it on your own. Let's go over it together now.

I know it might be hard to believe you can _____.
So, I'm going to show you just how easy it really is. Let's go over it together right now.

How "I" Do It (Content #2): Here's how I do it, step by step (just give a brief overview of the steps).

Here's exactly what I do every time:
Step 1:
Step 2:
Step 3:

Proof That It Works: Show your successful results, case studies, or other proof.

Here's how well it works for me . . .
But don't just take my word for it. Here's what my students have done . . .

Hook to Video #3: Get them excited for the next video.

Tomorrow, you'll discover _____.

VIDEO #3: OWNERSHIP EXPERIENCE

Future Pace Experience: Imagine what your life could be like if you commit to this program.

I want you to take a moment to imagine what would be different in your life if _____.
What possibilities would open up for you if _____?
How would you be different if _____?

How "YOU" Do It (Content #3): Imagine yourself doing this exact process. Here's what it would look like.

Now, imagine yourself doing _____, then _____, and finally _____.
Can you see yourself doing this?
In your mind's eye, it looks pretty simple, right?

Hinting to the Offer: Would you like the chance to learn in the fastest, easiest way possible?

We all know reality is usually a little more complicated than our imaginations. But I know this will change your life, and I want to see you succeed. That's why I'm going to help you _____.

Hook to Offer Video: In the next video, I'll show you how you can get results just like these.

Tomorrow, I'm going to show you the fastest and easiest way to _____.

Your success is closer than you know.

VIDEO #4: THE OFFER

Here's What I've Got: Explain the offer.

I really want to see you succeed. I've been where you are, and I know how hard it can seem. That's why I created _____.

Here's what you get . . .

Here's What You'll Do with It: Explain how it works.

Here's how each piece helps you move forward . . .

Here's What It'll Do for You: Explain the results.

When you follow the steps as I've outlined them, here's what you can expect . . .

Here's What You Need to Do Right Now: Explain how to order and what to expect next.

Just click the button below, and you'll be taken to a secure shopping page. In just three clicks from now, you'll be on your way to _____.

Let's Review: Product Launch Funnels are best used with warm or hot traffic. We usually send people to the videos from a link in an email—either to our own list or to an affiliate or JV partner's list. You break down your sales presentations into more digestible chunks, delivered over the course of a few days to build up excitement. You teach in the first three videos and then sell your product in the fourth.

Up Next: If you sell high-ticket coaching or consulting, you probably spend a ton of time on the phone with tire kickers and people who really aren't a good fit for your offer.

Wouldn't it be cool if you could just collect applications and pre-frame your high-ticket consulting clients to say *yes* before you even get on the phone with them?

Better yet, what if you didn't have to get on the phone with them at all, yet could still sell them on your offer? How cool would that be?

The secret is in the next chapter.

BACKEND FUNNEL

HIGH-TICKET, THREE-STEP APPLICATION

HIGH-TICKET, THREE-STEP APPLICATION FUNNEL

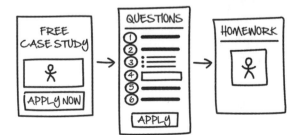

231

This funnel is a very simple process to qualify and pre-frame potential high-ticket consulting or coaching clients. For years we called all of our buyers and offered them coaching. The problem was it took sixty sales guys to contact all of our buyers. It cost me hundreds of thousands of dollars a month to weed through everyone and find the few who were interested. A few years ago, we decided to close down the call center and find a better way to sell our high-ticket coaching services. That's when this three-step application process was born. It has given us the ability to make almost as much gross revenue without having huge overhead. We can literally make as many sales with just two sales people as we could with sixty! Let me tell you how it works.

Step #1: You need to create a simple page that shares a case study video explaining the results your clients can get when they receive coaching from you. After watching the free case study video, potential clients click on the "apply now" button and are taken to an application designed to pre-qualify them as good prospects.

Step #2: The prospects fill out a full application, which serves two purposes. It helps your sales people learn about an applicant's business—

where they are now and what their business goals are for the future. More importantly, though, it pre-frames the prospect by getting them to sell you on why you should take them on as a coaching client. The application stage weeds out those who really aren't ready, so you are ONLY calling the prospects who are ready to start working with you. The application also pre-sells the program in the prospect's mind. After they finish the application, we take them to a "homework" page.

Step #3: The applicants follow the instructions on the homework page, all the while building an even stronger bond with the Attractive Character. My Inner Circle homework page includes three videos for applicants to watch. The first video is a short class with me teaching what it takes to succeed in this business. The second video tells the story of how my wife and I struggled to start our family. It explains exactly why I'm so passionate about helping business owners get their messages out into the world. (It's also a tear-jerker.) The third video is a series of case studies and testimonials about the coaching program itself.

Fig 20.3a: The homework page is an important
pre-frame step that helps make the final sale easier.

Another important function of the homework page is explaining what's going to happen next (the applicants will be contacted by one of our sales people) and offering a way to contact US by phone—if they just can't wait. My sales team is great at calling people quickly. But when people are in pain NOW, they often want to feel like they're being proactive. If someone is at that hyperactive buyer stage, I don't want them to have to wait for us to call. So, I give them a way to call us.

The sales script for selling the high-ticket item on the phone is pretty long and involved. Let's dive in and look at our script for selling high-ticket products.

HIGH-TICKET, TWO-STEP SCRIPT

Closing a high-end client takes more time and finesse than selling a simpler product. It's important to change the selling environment to a phone conversation; a live event or seminar environment could also work. Most prospects won't whip out a credit card and pay twenty-five thousand dollars based on a video sales letter alone. We have a very effective, high-end sales process, and I'm going to share the script with you here. It's much more involved than the other scripts we've covered in this book so far. In fact, the entire process can take from seventy-five minutes to two hours. If you're interested in learning the finer points and details involved in selling with this process, you can learn more at www.highticketsecrets.com.

My team uses a two-step script because it's really the most effective way to close a high-end ticket sale over the phone. You will need two different people to make a sale using this process: the setter and the closer. Using two sales people provides consistency in your sales. When you find the right people and they follow the script, it works, day in and day out. You should not be the one selling directly on the phone; you're too close to the outcome emotionally, and it's just bad positioning.

Instead, two sales people work together to close a new client. The setter gathers basic information on the prospect, draws out his emotions, and identifies the prospect's pain and goals. Once that is done, the setter gets off the phone and has the closer call the applicant back. The closer magnifies the pain, gets the prospect to sell himself on why he is a good fit for the program, and then provides the solution.

THE SET SCRIPT

Introduction: For setters, the goal here is to introduce themselves in a low-key way and have a natural conversation with the prospect. The setter is getting to know the prospect and pulling out any emotions related to the topic you're discussing. They must find out where the prospect is right now and *how he feels* about where he is.

Questions: Then the setter should focus on finding out where the prospect wants to be. What are his hopes and dreams? What's the real reason, deep down, that he wants those things? He may want to make a hundred thousand a year—that's great. But why? What would that money allow him to do? Quit his current job? Stay home with his kids? Buy a boat and sail around the world? Buy his aging parents a home? Finally show his ex-wife that he's worth something after all? The setter has to find out the *why*. That's where you'll find the emotions. Remember, people buy based on emotion first, then they rationalize the decision with logic.

You've probably heard sales advice saying you need to get to a buyer's emotions, but I find many people just don't know how to do that. You hook the emotions by asking questions. Always ask additional questions. Does the prospect have kids? Great! How old are they? What are their names? If you know the prospect wants to homeschool his kids, ask why. How would it feel to know he had the freedom to teach his kids any way he wanted? Follow-up questions help you hook into emotions. What would it mean to the prospect if he could buy that new house for his parents? How would he feel standing on a boat in the Caribbean, totally free of debt and worry? Help the prospect paint a picture of the *feelings* behind his dreams. You can get all this information with a few questions; within five minutes, the setter knows exactly why the prospect is going to buy this program. He also knows the hot buttons to focus on.

The setter should ask the prospect, "What's holding you back? Why haven't you achieved your dreams already?" You'll probably hear some variation of *I don't know how*. The prospect doesn't know how to build a business online. Or, he may say he doesn't have time—which is really saying he doesn't know how to build a business in five hours a week. He may say it is because he doesn't have money—which is really saying he doesn't know how to build a business using other people's money. Once the prospect realizes it's simply a lack of knowledge blocking his success—and that you can provide him with that knowledge—ask him this question: *If you knew how to build a business in just five hours a week, would you do it?* Of course, he is going to say yes! He has just started to sell himself on purchasing your product, your knowledge.

The setter cannot move forward with the script until he understands the prospect's emotional hot buttons. The prospect must also admit he doesn't know what he is doing (in some form or another) when it comes to building a business. He must realize he needs help.

Blast: Give Him a Taste of What You Offer: Don't go into great detail about the program; that's what he's buying. But the setter should give him an idea of what he could discover or get done.

Now, obviously, it's impossible to work with everyone who applies/buys our information . . . so I'm here to weed out those who aren't ready and find the right people to work with one-on-one. I understand you don't know how to build a business in five hours a week. And I don't know, but maybe we can help. Let me explain what we do here . . .

Next, ask a critical question to get the prospect to sell himself. Use a pivotal question that will bring home all the reasons he needs to pull out his credit card at the end of the conversation.

Let me ask you this . . . if you could work one-on-one with Russell Brunson or someone like him . . . do you think you'd be successful?

(Absolutely!)

How come?

Here's why this is so important: I can talk for hours about how great our program is and all the reasons the prospect should buy . . . but it might be a lie. If HE tells me all the reasons he'd be successful with our program . . . then it's the truth because he believes it. When the setter gets him to explain all the reasons he'd be successful, sales become easy.

Ask: *How come? Why would working with Russell Brunson help you be successful?*

Then, the setter must shut up! Don't talk. Let the prospect talk.

Once he gives the reasons, the setter should repeat them back and confirm his beliefs.

So, if I gave you the chance to work with Russell Brunson, you believe you'd be successful? (Yes!)

If you had the opportunity to work with Russell Brunson, you could get (fill in what they want)?

If you had the opportunity to work with Russell Brunson, you'd know how to get there?

Next, get the prospect to sell himself and tell the setter why you should work with him.

Why do you think you'd be a good candidate for this program?

Posture: To set up the closer as the expert, the setter should say the following:

Now, I'm not personally an expert at building businesses online in five hours a week. My job is simply to find the people who are qualified to be part of this program. If I feel good about you, I'll turn you over to our Program Director (the closer). *He is the one to decide who will be the right fit for our program.*

Before I do that, I need to find out a little more about you and fill out a short profile. I need to understand where you are right now professionally and financially. Then I need to find out more specifics about where you want to be in the future. All this information will help us determine if you're going to be a good candidate.

Is it alright if I ask you a few questions?

(Sure . . .)

The setter has just asked for (and gotten) permission to ask just about anything.

Probe: Collect Financial Information: Your setter is going to start asking some pretty personal questions next and is going to fill out a form with the information. You want people to answer quickly, without getting too emotional. Start by asking about age, marital status, highest level of education, and things like that.

Then the setter must be sure to ask, *Is there anyone else involved in your business—a spouse or financial partner?* If so, get the other party on the phone, too, right then and there. It's a waste of time to keep going through the presentation if you don't have all the decision makers present.

The goal of this next set of questions is to find out the prospect's financial status and whether you really can help.

Finding Credit: Your setter is going to find out details about the prospect's credit situation.

How would you rate your credit right now? Why?

If Russell Brunson were to write a check and pay off all your debt, how much would that be?

Of that debt, how much is major credit card debt?

What's the total amount of combined credit that's been extended to you? (Subtract total debt from combined credit extended, and you find out how much he has available.)

You're looking for more available credit than the program costs. It's also helpful to get him to talk about his credit balances to show that you're really trying to help pay those off—not add to them. The prospect might need to take one step back to take ten steps forward, but ultimately we know a program like this can help him pay off all the debt and achieve financial freedom.

The setter should also ask if the prospect has any savings accounts or investments. Does he own his own home or rent? What about retirement accounts?

Goals: Talking About a Prospect's Short-Term Goals: Your setter is still asking questions and getting the prospect to sell himself on the program.

What would be an optimal situation in six months? Where would you want your business in six months?

How long have you been trying to do _____? How successful have you been?

In twelve months, where do you want to be? What would make you feel good?

So, in working one-on-one with Russell Brunson . . . do you think you could achieve these goals? Can you see yourself achieving them? How come?

Commitments: Get Four Commitments: Now the setter is getting the prospect to declare himself a good candidate. He is publicly stating he is the kind of person who takes action and finishes what he starts. Once he does this, his brain will have a really hard time reversing that declaration and talking himself out of the purchase.

You look like a potential candidate for me to recommend to my director. Before I can make the recommendation and turn you over to him, there are four commitments that must be agreeable to you.

1. You must have a minimum time commitment of _____ per week. Can you do that?

2. We need people who are coachable and willing to learn and follow the advice of our experts. Can you do that? Why are you coachable?

3. We're looking for people who can start today. We want quick decision makers. When do you think is the best time to start working on _____ (his goals)?

You want to hear some version of "right now."

Great. If it looks like this is a fit for both of us, is there anything that would hold you back from getting started today?

4. We want to teach you the concept of using OPM (other people's money) to invest in _____. Are you familiar with this idea? Would you like to learn more about it?

Explain how to use the bank's money (credit cards) as a short-term leveraging tool to invest in growing his business or reaching his goals.

We have two levels in this program: _____ and _____. (Lower price and higher price.)

How much are you comfortable investing to get your business started today? Why would you choose that amount?

Now put him on hold while you go talk to your "director." Discuss the candidate with the closer. If you feel like he would be a good fit for your program, and someone you'd like to work with, then come back to the call.

Let me have you write down my director's name; it's _____. I'm so happy he's available to talk with you personally, because he is an expert at _____. Most importantly, his job is to make sure we have the right kind of people on our team. So, I want you to understand this is not for everybody. Please don't be offended if he doesn't offer you a slot. Okay?

He's in a meeting right now, but he said he'll be happy to call you back in five or ten minutes.

He wanted me to give you a little exercise to go through while you are waiting. I know we've talked about your goals, but he'd like you to write them down for yourself. Write down a six- to twelve-month financial goal. Next, write down three things you want besides money.

Okay? Great! My director will call you shortly.

THE CLOSE SCRIPT

This script for the closer is very similar to the Set Script. You want to reinforce the candidate's decisions in his mind. The closer will go through the same questions as in the introduction, but perhaps worded a little differently. Get the candidate to picture exactly what life will be like after he has success with your program.

Why are you serious about _____ right now?

How long have you been thinking about _____?

What's the biggest thing that's held you back from _____?

What are you looking to do in six months? What would that do for you?

What are you hoping for in twelve months? What would that do for you?

How about in five years? What would your lifestyle be like?

Then you want the prospect to connect you with his dreams.

If you have the chance to work with someone like Russell Brunson, how would that make a difference in your life? Anything else?

Next, the closer goes through the four commitments again.

It's my job to find only the very best people for this program. It's not for everybody, and I only want people on board if I know they have what it takes to be successful. So I'm going to ask you a series of questions, and these are things you're either committed to or you're not. So, they are simple yes or no answers. Is that something you're willing to do?

Don't move on if you're not getting the answers you're looking for. Either back track to find out why the prospect isn't committed or get off the phone because he is not a likely close.

Time: Explain the Time Commitment

Are you able to commit to _____ hours per week? (Yes or no.)

Decision Making: Explain the Decision Commitment

Opportunities don't wait around. Making decisions is very important. Do you see anything that would hold you back from making a decision to work with Russell Brunson today? (Yes or no.)

Resources: Investment Commitment

Write this number down: _____.

Now, as long as you see the value, and the program meets all your goals, is there any reason you can think of that would keep you from investing _____ today? (Yes or no.)

If the setter and the closer have done all the previous steps correctly and the prospect says you or your product/service is the next best thing to sliced bread, then suddenly the price tag isn't such a big deal anymore. It's all about setting things up in the beginning to keep him from objecting to the money at this step.

Knowledge: Teachability

My main concern with taking on students is that they are teachable. They must be willing to learn and then implement what they've learned so they are successful. Do you feel like you're that kind of person? (Yes or no.)

How come?

So if someone could show you how to do _____, you would be successful? (Yes or no.)

What's Included: What the Prospect Gets When He Signs Up Today

We're going to give you everything you need to be successful and avoid mistakes. Your coach will help you work at your own speed.

Now, simply list out exactly what buyers get with the product or program.

Close: Finalizing the Sale

This is probably the most important question . . .

Why do you feel like you are a good candidate for this program?

The prospect is selling himself *again* on how he will be successful if he is accepted. Then all that's left to do is take his credit card information. Instead of you asking for the sale, he is asking you to *let him* buy. Do you see the subtle distinction there?

Sales become easy when he tells you (or your setter/closer) why he needs your help.

Okay, that's the whole two-step script for the setter and the closer. Again, I strongly recommend you listen to this script in action to gain a better understanding of each step. Just go to www.highticketsecrets.com.

Let's Review: When selling high-ticket coaching and consulting programs, it's important to weed out people quickly if they aren't going to be a good fit. That way, you can spend more time with the people you can really help. The application and homework pages pre-frame and pre-sell the prospect on all the reasons he should sign up—instead of worrying about all the reasons he shouldn't sign up.

When there's twenty-five, fifty, or a hundred thousand dollars on the line at the end of a sales call, you want to make sure you're following a proven plan. The most effective way I've found to close high-ticket sales is to hire two commission-based sales people and have them use the two-step script outlined in this chapter.

Up Next: Now that you have learned how all seven core funnels work and the scripts we use at each level, I want to show you how simple it can be to build out these funnels. I am going to give you a quick tutorial on how to use ClickFunnels.com to build out any funnel you can dream of.

click funnels

One of the first questions people ask me after they learn about my seven core funnels is this: *But, Russell, there's so much technology involved . . . how do I create all the web pages and make sure they're connected together correctly?* I don't want technology to hold anyone back from building a more successful business, so I want to officially introduce you to ClickFunnels. It can be your new best friend and take care of most of the tech stuff for you.

This section is not meant to be a full tutorial on how to use ClickFunnels. The first step I go through when creating any funnel is to decide which type of funnel I'm going to create. Is this a frontend funnel? Is it a middle-of-the-Value-Ladder funnel or a backend funnel? After I know which type of funnel, then I decide which one of the seven core funnels offers the best way to sell this product.

Then I usually get in front of a whiteboard and sketch out each of the steps this funnel will require. Remember the seven phases of a funnel and also the twenty-three building blocks I explained? Am I going to use a quiz to pre-frame this funnel, or just start with a squeeze page? What price will I set for my frontend offer? Will I use an order form bump? How many upsells will I have? Will I add any downsells if the customer says no to one of my upsells?

Next, I want to map out my follow-up sequence. Who is my Attractive Character? How do I want to flesh out that character in my emails? What will I say in each email in my Soap Opera Sequence? What types of messages do I want to send out in my Seinfeld emails?

I then sketch it out like this:

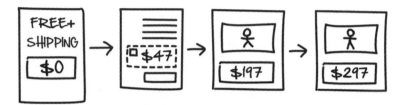

Fig 21.2: First, we draw out the flow of the funnel.
Then we set everything up with a few clicks inside ClickFunnels.

After I have a visual representation of what I want to build, then I can log in to ClickFunnels.com and let the magic begin. We've made ClickFunnels easy enough that a CEO could use it, but also powerful enough that your web and tech guys will love it.

Step #1: Pick which type of funnel you want to build.

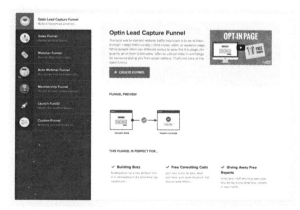

Fig 21.3: The first step in ClickFunnels is choosing what type of funnel you want to build.

Step #2: Choose which template you want to use at each step in the funnel, or you can custom design your own templates from scratch. My team has dozens of proven templates that we've perfected over the years for each of these steps, so it would be hard to go wrong if you stick with these.

Fig 21.4: Step two is choose your web page template.

Step #3: After you've picked the template designs for each step, finalize the funnel and you will be able to see your entire sales funnel at a glance.

Fig 21.5: Once you've finalized your funnel, the page templates are set up and all your analytics and stats are available on the dashboard.

Step #4: Now you can go in and edit the copy, add your videos, integrate with your email auto-responder, and set up your order forms on each page.

Fig 21.6: Text, video, buttons, order forms—
all areas of the template are customizable.

After that's finished, you'll see that the sales funnel you sketched out on the whiteboard has now come to life. You can start driving traffic and getting results in record time! Isn't that exciting?! While this once took our team of experts two to four weeks to create, we can now create everything in ClickFunnels in about an hour!

If you don't have your ClickFunnels account yet, you can get a free, two-week trial at www.ClickFunnels.com.

Also, if you want to see how to build out any of the specific funnels in this book, you can see a live demo at www.DotComSecretsBook.com/resources/cfdemo.

CONCLUSION:

IGNITE

Phew!

Right now you're probably feeling a bit overwhelmed. This book is not exactly what I would consider light reading. You've just concluded a full-on immersion course in high-level Internet marketing strategy, and you should feel proud of yourself.

Being overwhelmed is actually a good thing because even though you feel like all that information is a big, jumbled MESS upstairs, your brain is subconsciously making connections. Right now, without you consciously doing anything, it's figuring out which competitors you might want to research. It's strategizing about what your Value Ladder will look like and what types of sales funnels you will use to ascend people on your Value Ladder. All this is happening, even though you might feel overwhelmed.

Pretty cool, huh?

Your most important tools are the silly little diagrams I've given you in each chapter. After all this information has a chance to sink in for a day or so, go back to the images and see how much of the entire chapter you can recall. I think you'll surprise yourself. And if you do forget one of the concepts, you can always go back through the book and re-read the sections you want to remember.

So, what in the world should you work on first? Here's what I recommend:

1. Decide who you want to serve. Who are your ideal clients?
2. Create your bait, and do it quickly. Don't overthink it or try for perfection here.
3. Figure out your Value Ladder. What can you offer above and beyond what you currently do? Go create those things.
4. Start building out your funnels, one at a time.

This book is a playbook. Don't just read it once and go on with business as usual. Keep it handy, and refer to it often. Once you get your first couple of funnels working, I would strongly suggest spending a week or two implementing one of the secrets you learned here. Then move on to another secret and another. When you've run through all of them, go back, and do it again! Continue to improve.

IGNITE YOUR BUSINESS

Many people who read this book before it went to print wanted me to look at their ideas personally, including their startups, or their existing businesses and sales funnels. I did just that for a few friends and was able to identify the holes that were keeping them from growing as fast as they wanted. I suggested the simple tweaks needed to implement these

DotComSecrets you've just learned about. We were able to see dramatic increases almost overnight in each of these companies.

That's what I love so much about the things you've learned in this book. They are all simple concepts that you can apply without too much effort, but the results from each of these tweaks can double or triple your sales almost overnight.

Once this book is available to millions, I know it's going to be much harder to accommodate everyone who wants more personalized help. So I created something special just for the readers of this book. I've opened up space in our DotComSecrets Ignite program so that I can personally look at your current funnels, spend an hour with you on the phone, and then have my team work with you for a full year to implement the changes you need to make.

If you'd be interested in being part of Ignite, then I want to invite you to apply with me personally. You can apply here:

http://Ignite.DotComSecrets.com

After you apply, someone on my team will give you a call and explain the Ignite program to see if it's a good fit. If it is, then we could actually be talking together less than a week from right now.

And with that . . .

I will end this book.

Thank you so much for reading, and I wish you all the success you can dream of . . .

Russell Brunson